Managing Success

A Manager's Guide to Effective Employee Relationships

Managing Success

A Manager's Guide to Effective Employee Relationships

Jeremy Henderson, MHR

Jungle Red Communication, LLC

Jungle Red Communication
1001 46th St., Suite 313
Emeryville, CA 94608

Contents

Prologue

I set out to write this book after nearly 20 years of listening to employees talk about their bad bosses. As a human relations leader, I've heard some of the nastiest, craziest, and most absurd stories that are unfortunately all too common. So as you read this book, you will not find a lot of research recited here, because this book was written mainly on the basis of observation, experience, and common sense.

The book began as an advice guide for new managers, but I quickly realized that the types of managerial secrets I share within are right for anyone who performs a managerial role. As such, this book is for anyone who is managing other humans, wants to get better at it, and is open to receiving help in doing so.

It is critically important that you realize up front that management is a learned skill, not an innate ability. Find managers who you think do an exceptional job, and they will tell you that they have failed in their role more times than they have succeeded. But when you practice the art of management through the principles of human relations, all of which are presented within this book, you have a far better chance of success.

Management is also not for the faint of heart. If you feel like you need someone to hold your hand, brush your hair, and call you pretty, please put this book down now and run to the self-help section of the bookstore. There is a book there waiting for you. We guarantee it! This book is going to require you to take some risks, to take an honest look at yourself and your behavior, and to muster up the courage you will need to change and grow and commit to managing effective employee relationships.

Now here's the good news. Once you have made your way through this guide, you'll have a much better understanding of yourself as a manager. And with better understanding comes a consciousness that will lead you from the managerial practices you employ today, to those that can help you achieve amazing results in the future with your employees.

This book is dedicated to the best teachers in the world.

Thank you for your faith in me:

Keith for the love
Kim for the practice
Ann for the inspiration
George for the knowledge
Melanie for the opportunity
Julia for the mentorship
Erin for the spark

Managing Success

A Manager's Guide to Effective Employee Relationships

Effective Relationships Begin with You

Congratulations! All of your hard work, talent, and dedication have paid off. You've finally become a manager!

But once the excitement of your new promotion wears off, you may find yourself wondering what ever made you think this was a good idea in the first place? Do you have experience managing people? Did anyone ever teach you to be a manager? What if you can't do it? What if taking on this challenge and managing others is a terrible career mistake?

If you find yourself in exactly this kind of panic, we're here to tell you that there are real, concrete, and learnable reasons why some managers succeed and other managers don't. In fact, we're so confident that you can learn to become a great manager that we've written a book to help you achieve that goal.

Commitment to Being a Loved Manager

To become an effective manager, you are going to have to dedicate yourself to learning the art of understanding behaviors. Then, you must commit yourself to putting what you've learned into practice every day, in every way you can. You can't just be a good manager for a few hours a day or get to it later when it is more convenient for you to practice. Why? Because your team will be miserable and you'll fall flat on your face trying to produce even the smallest results.

Truly successful managers of people recognize that the most important part of their role is first and foremost a commitment to the people they're managing.

Some companies will reward you for being a hierarchical control freak first and a good manager of humans second. But, how does that serve you or your team? It doesn't. As that famous song so eloquently says, "People who need people are the luckiest people in the world." Interestingly, the same thing goes for managers: You need the people on your team and the people on your team need you, and they need you to be approachable, honest, appropriately transparent in your communications with them, and above all, human.

So as you embark on your journey to become the best manager you have ever known in your entire life, remember that each and every person you encounter is indeed an emotional being just like yourself. And when you do commit to managing your team in a way that is first and foremost emotionally responsible, the end result is that your career will soar. You will be looked at not just as an incredibly skilled leader, but you will also be put on a platform as one of the most successful managers in your entire company. You can do it! You can be the most successful manager you and everyone around you have ever had the pleasure of working with. Again, it only takes your sincere commitment to people and dedicated practice of effective human relations principles.

According to Professor of Management Studies Henry Mintzberg of McGill University, "Management is, above all, a practice where art, science, and craft meet." (Leaders)

Avoid Bad Boss Behavior

You've probably heard the expression that people quit their boss, not their job. Well, it's true. Bad bosses are the number one reason employees quit. That's just common sense though, right? There isn't a soul in the world that will stay in a job for years on end with a bad boss.

There are a number of different types of bad bosses that exist, as well as good managers. The first step to knowing the difference between the two is to dive deep into the types of behaviors they each exhibit.

To help you identify the behavior a bad boss typically exhibits, we've created bad boss archetypes as symbols to help illustrate and clearly articulate exactly why these behaviors are bad.

- *The Bully*—Bullies aren't just found on schoolyards; they are front and center in business, as are their techniques to get ahead. Do a quick Google search and you will find that there is a lot of information that points out that those who are meaner tend to get promoted faster than those who approach work in an amiable fashion. Well, we say "no" to Bullies.

- *The Pacifier*—Everyone had a "bubbie" at some point in his or her life, but rarely do we want one in the office. The Pacifier is a bad boss who takes on the parental role and thinks his or her job is to raise employees, rather than lead the team to high productivity.

- *The Ostrich*—The Ostrich is one heck of a large, fast bird and is famous for burying its head in the sand when the going gets rough. There are a lot of bad bosses who will do the same thing; when the going gets rough, these bosses will barricade themselves in their offices and wait for the storm to pass.

- *The Martyr*—Just like Joan of Arc, a Martyr is a bad boss who is entirely overworked, never asks for help or delegates tasks, and always lets you know about it. These types of bosses are usually known for "taking one for the team," and often their employees pity rather than respect them.

- *The Sleeper*—Probably the hardest bad boss to identify, the Sleeper is the boss that you just don't understand. He or she doesn't really work to achieve the company strategy, nor does the Sleeper contribute much of anything that really matters, while simultaneously insisting that he or she is "right." As a result, Sleepers rarely get any traction for the work they are attempting to push forward.

There are a lot of ways to describe bad bosses and these are just a few of the most common archetypes that most of us will experience at one time or another. But the point here is to remember that we are all human and we all have valuable contributions to make, regardless of bad behavior. If we can work to understand the types of bad managers that we've experienced, or even the bad behavior that they tend to exhibit, then we can also find a way to help move from the negative side of management to the positive side, which is where your career will soar as a manager of people and your team will truly succeed.

Aspire to Be a Good Manager

And just like there are negative managerial archetypes that exist, there are also archetypes that exist for good managers. Read this set of good manager archetypes and see which ones resonate most with you.

- *The Strategist*—The Strategist doesn't waste time with negative emotions or spinning the team's proverbial wheels. Instead, the Strategist is the type of manager who focuses on helping the team to achieve its goals as a significant contribution to the company's overall business success. The Strategist puts the right people on the right jobs, ensures that team projects are rewarding, helps team members expand their skills, and fuels each individual's contributions to the collective team's success.

- *The Mentor*—The Mentor is arguably the best type of boss an employee can have. Why? Because the Mentor will push you to take on new tasks that you would have never thought possible, while giving you the tools and support you need to ensure success. The Mentor offers up his or her past experiences so that you can avoid common pitfalls, but also lets you have a few minor failures along the way so that you can learn firsthand from the mistakes that we all make.

- *The Giraffe*—The exact opposite management style from the Ostrich, the Giraffe keeps his or her head very high in the sky, focused on what's coming next for the team. Because they can see so far ahead, Giraffes can coordinate better for everyone on the ground and make great strides toward the team's success. The Giraffe also lowers his or her head to ground level to set the entire team's expectations, as well as to keep himself or herself grounded.

- *The Champion*—The Champion is also an exceptionally strong type of manager. This managerial archetype is typically characterized by the manager who will go into battle to bring the team's best interests up the chain, as well as serve as a cheerleader and motivational speaker for each and every member of the group. The Champion gets things done at the top, with peers, and removes obstacles that may stand in his or her employees' way.

- *The Communicator*—Who doesn't like to have a manager who openly and honestly communicates the ins and outs of the business? The communicator is the type of manager who focuses on keeping every single person up to speed about the work that the team needs to get done. The communicator doesn't worry about repeating what he or she has said over and over again because sometimes the team just needs to hear it frequently to remind them of what they're doing and why they're doing it.

As a manager, you have the unique opportunity to choose the type of style that you will use now and into the future. It's all up to you. You can mix and match the best of each style to create one that is uniquely your own. But no one can make the choice for you. You can choose to have a terrible impact on the people around you, or you can choose to be the type of manager that people will follow even during the toughest of times.

Now that you've had the opportunity to read about the different types of managers that exist in the workplace, it's time to figure out which type of manager you are today and which type of manager you would ideally like to be in the future. To get to the answer, you have to be completely honest with yourself about your own behaviors.

The truth is it can be difficult to see ourselves clearly. And as typical as that may be, the inability to see our own shortcomings can get in the way of becoming a good manager. If you can't be honest with yourself or you are not sure if you are being honest with yourself, ask members of your team, or even your manager, to give input into the types of behaviors they see you expressing most frequently.

If you don't feel comfortable asking others for input, then the chart below may help you to understand the types of behaviors that stick out between bad bosses and good managers.

	Bad Boss Behavior	*Good Manager Behavior*
Bully vs. Communicator	• Screams and hollers • Aggressive behavior • Intimidates for results	• Meets regularly to update team on programs, projects, and policies • Invites collaboration • Finds ways for the team to proactively express their needs, skills, and ability to work together
Pacifier vs. Mentor	• Treats the team like children • Gives rewards to calm the	• Invites you to take on new challenges • Gives you the benefit of his or

	group • Insists everything is okay when indeed, it isn't	her experience • Lets you learn from mistakes without blame, shame, or punishment
Ostrich vs. Giraffe	• Always wears rose-colored glasses • Stays in his or her office with the door closed • Doesn't get involved in conflict	• Consistently looks 2 to 3 months ahead • Coordinates team skills and resources exceptionally well • Solid vision of teamwork
Martyr vs. Champion	• Takes on assignments that are too challenging • Works too much and tells you about it—often! • Doesn't delegate	• Positively represents the team to higher-ups • Takes responsibility for the team's failures • Gives others credit for team successes
Sleeper vs. Strategist	• Gives assignments that don't make sense • Insists on projects that are inconsistent with the company's	• Focused on company strategy • Aligns team goals to company strategy • Positively focuses on individual

	goals • Is unclear about the direction that should be taken	contributions to goals

It is critically important that you figure out what type of manager you are very quickly and before you try to improve your skills. To do that, create a base point from which you can grow.

If you're having trouble seeing yourself in any of these archetypes, it's likely that you need to ask yourself some hard-hitting questions that will help you go deeper into who you are in a way that is honest and meaningful. Remember, this assessment is all about helping you to be the best manager you can be. To determine your primary archetype, you will need to continue to have a very honest and open dialogue with yourself so that you can indeed achieve the type of success in your managerial career that you deserve.

Below are a few tough questions that may help you identify with one or more of the above archetypes. You will likely have behaviors that are both associated with the bad boss archetypes and the good manager archetypes. The key is to identify those behaviors that are working for you as a manager and those that are not.

The point of this exercise is to simply get you thinking about in which end of the managerial spectrum—from bad boss to good manager—your skills already lie. The exercise should get you to consider your behaviors and how your team perceives your behaviors.

Are You a Bad Boss or Good Manager?

On a scale of one (rarely) to five (always), rate yourself on the following statements.

1. When I need to get something done, I pull together the team to talk about the best solution.

2. I regularly ask members of the team to take on new challenges, and then support their success with the project.

3. I understand the strengths and weaknesses of each and every individual on my team, and coordinate assignments so that each person's strengths are being used consistently for the betterment of our group.

4. My manager believes that each member of my team is a rock star.

5. Each member of my team understands the company strategy, our team's goals, and how their work contributes to our collective success.

Now, add up the total number of points that you earned. Based on your points, you can classify yourself as a good manager, a bad boss, or a little bit of both:

- 20-25—You're doing great! It is likely that you are doing a lot of things right as a manager and can work on making yourself an even stronger manager as your skills grow.

- 11-19—Room to Grow. You probably experience intermittent success as a manager and can choose to either get better by focusing on developing and consistently applying good managerial practices or allow yourself to slip into the bad boss category, should you not elect to improve.

- 5-10—Yikes! You are probably a bad boss already—the type of manager most of us do not want to be around, let alone work for. Step up and make the changes you need to become a good manager.

Again, you have to know where you are today so that you know where you can go tomorrow in the development of your people management skills. So, be honest, be clear, and document the type of manager that you are today.

Have Clear Values and Honest Motivations

Although many of us rarely spend time thinking about what our values are, each of us has a set. The expression of our values helps others to know what is important to us and give clues about how to walk well by our side. As such, values play a big role in building effective employee relationships. Your values come from the experiences that you have had with your family, as a kid in school, in the workplace, within your community, online and on the streets, with politics and religion, and much more. The point here is that your values serve as a guide post for you on a day-to-day basis.

You make decisions about how you manage your team based on your own personal values, rather than the values of the company, the collective values of your team, or perhaps even the values that individuals on your team hold. As such, the values that you have acquired have a much bigger impact on those around you than you realize.

You can use your values to effectively manage your team when you are very clear about which values are useful for you to express in the workplace. When you are conscious of your values and clear about how you apply your values in the workplace, you will automatically become a better manager, and your career will advance accordingly.

Values are commonly accepted as a manifestation of virtues, which vary within cultures, societies, and religions around the world. Values are a much longer list of virtues, are more actionable, and tend to serve as the tenets through which we make decisions about what is right and what is wrong. Values guide and inform our actions as managers.

Below, you'll find a short list of values. It is by no means exhaustive. Some of the values will have little to no meaning to you, while others may evoke a negative response. Still others may jump out at you and truly express the type of person that you strive to be. Spend a few moments reading the below list of values and see if a certain number of values pop up as important for you. Circle those values. Explore further and add values that are not listed on the chart but are important to you. Then, see if there is any relationship between the types of values that you have indicated and your managerial style. (Pavlina)

Short List of Values			
Acceptance	Empathy	Ingenuity	Resilience
Accessibility	Encourage-ment	Inspiration	Satisfaction
Activeness	Endurance	Integrity	Security
Adaptability	Energy	Intelligence	Self-control
Adroitness	Enjoyment	Intensity	Selflessness
Adventure	Depth	Intimacy	Self-reliance
Affection	Desire	Investing	Sensitivity
Affluence	Discipline	Joy	Sexuality
Agility	Discovery	Learning	Sharing
Alertness	Discretion	Liberation	Shrewdness
Altruism	Diversity	Liberty	Sincerity
Ambition	Dominance	Liveliness	Skillfulness
Assurance	Dynamism	Logic	Solidarity
Audacity	Excitement	Longevity	Solitude
Availability	Exhilaration	Love	Soundness
Awareness	Exuberance	Loyalty	Speed
Awe	Fairness	Majesty	Spirit
Balance	Family	Making a difference	Spirituality
Beauty	Fascination	Mastery	Spontaneity
Being the			Spunk

best	Fashion	Maturity	
Belonging	Ferocity	Meekness	
Boldness	Fidelity	Mellowness	
Bravery	Fierceness	Mindfulness	Strength
Brilliance	Financial	Modesty	Structure
Buoyancy	Firmness	Motivation	Success
Calmness	Fitness	Neatness	Support
Candor	Frugality	Nerve	Supremacy
Carefulness	Fun	Obedience	Surprise
Celebrity	Gallantry	Openness	Sympathy
Certainty	Generosity	Optimism	Synergy
Challenge	Gentility	Order	Teamwork
Chastity	Giving	Organization	Temperance
Clarity	Grace	Originality	Thankfulness
Cleanliness	Gratitude	Passion	Thrift
Cleverness	Growth	Peace	Tidiness
Closeness	Guidance	Perfection	Timeliness
Comfort	Happiness	Perkiness	Tranquility
Composure	Harmony	Persistence	Trust
Conviction	Health	Philanthropy	Truth
Conviviality	Heart	Piety	Unflappability
Courage	Helpfulness	Playfulness	Usefulness
Courtesy	Heroism	Pleasantness	Wealth
Craftiness	Holiness	Precision	Wisdom
Creativity	Honesty	Privacy	Wonder
Cunning	Hospitality	Proactivity	Youthfulness
Education	Humility	Purity	Zeal

Now that you have identified those values that speak to you and are the most important values by which you live your life, take some time to identify those values that you find to be of lowest importance to you. By knowing the values that you feel are most and least important, you will be able to identify those people with whom you share a great number of values, as well as those people who tend to get under your skin because you find their values to be insignificant or unimportant. It doesn't mean that your values are right and their values are wrong; it just means that we all have different experiences that lead us to our values.

As a manager, understanding your values will help you to have a great deal of confidence in how you run your team. If you do not know which values you find to be most important in your life, then you will tend not to know what to stand up for when something "wrong" comes across your desk. You can use your values as the basis for your managerial decisions, such as hiring, firing, compensation, promotions, performance reviews, and more. In addition, as a manager, it is very important to have a diversity of values represented on your team so that you can fuel collaboration, innovation, and creativity in a way that would not be possible if every single one of the people in your organization thinks and acts exactly the same.

Get Clear on Your Managerial Motivation

Just like your personal values, it is exceedingly important as a manager to clearly understand what motivates you and to determine if your motivations are consistent with your personal values. Our motivations are often more apparent than our values. People know when your motivations are not admirable. With that in mind, having motivations that promote the common good will benefit you in the development of effective employee relations.

According to acclaimed author Napoleon Hill, author of *How to Sell Your Way Through Life*, there are nine key motivators to which humans respond. While the essence of his theory is represented in the motivators below, our definitions here don't match up exactly; but he sure does deserve the credit for the list. (Hill)

- *Self-preservation*—Arguably one of the most common motivators in business today, self-preservation is essentially the instinct to keep oneself alive. If you are intrinsically motivated by self-preservation, you likely find yourself avoiding conflict and quickly fulfilling the requests of those higher up in your organization without consideration for your team's welfare.

- *Financial gain*—We are taught that money can solve pretty much any issue; so if we have a great deal of money in our lives, then our issues tend to be reduced. That in itself is a powerful motivator, and many people seek to earn as much money as possible in order to create a great sense of security. If you are motivated by financial gain, it is likely that you focus on earning commissions, increasing your paycheck, receiving, bigger bonuses, earning stock, etc. In other words, you focus almost exclusively on the financial outcomes of the work that you perform.

- *Love*—A core emotion, love is the strong affection and personal attachment that you may feel for someone or something. As a motivator, however, love can fuel your productivity because love inspires you to ensure that someone or something succeeds. Love is optimistic—if love is your motivation, you're likely to believe that everything will work out as long as you are committed. As this is a core emotion, we will also deal with love in a later chapter.

- *Sexuality*—Although sexual harassment laws around the globe have tried to completely wipe out sexuality in the workplace, it's been a futile endeavor. Essentially, sexuality is how people experience themselves as sexual beings. Sexuality does not mean the act of sexual intercourse, however. If sexuality is a motivator for you, you may find yourself very interested in the physical make up or manifestation of a man or woman. You may be inclined to hire only men or only women. Or you may be keenly interested in those types of affinity groups that are focused on certain sexualities or related groups, such as gender-affiliated organizations for women in the workplace, gay/lesbian/bisexual affinity groups in the office, or a sincere commitment to the old boys' club.

- *Power and fame*—Many people will say that money is the root of all evil, but that may not be entirely true. The desire for power and fame can overshadow someone's need for money, because when one is famous or holds a great deal of power they are not bound by the limits of common man or woman. As a matter of fact, the more power or fame that an employee has, the more the person has a chance of becoming an idolized.

- *Fear*—Fear is another core emotion that we will deal with later in this book. As a motivator, however, fear can manifest itself as a great deal of anxiety or unpleasant feelings of apprehension caused by a sense that danger is near. Fear is one of the principle ways companies have of managing employees. In most companies, fear is the instantaneous and involuntary response for an employee who makes a mistake, is the cause of the major issue, or is threatened with termination.

- *Revenge*—It's sad to say, but too many people are motivated by revenge, which tends to stem from some early childhood training relating to that Biblical measure of justice, "an eye for an eye." If revenge is your main source of motivation, you're likely to be someone who plots out ways to get a colleague fired, make a coworker look bad in retaliation for having made you look bad, or withhold rewards for a job well done because the person outshines you.

- *Freedom of body and soul*—Increasingly, many people are motivated by not being weighed down with rules, guidelines, policies, and procedures—or even working for one company for all that long. Having freedom of body and soul means that you prefer to be unchained, and you're probably not the right person to be tied down.

- *Desire to create or build*—There are a good number of managers out there who find themselves motivated by a desire to create or build. These are the managers who probably don't stay for a long period of time at any one company, but join the organization to create a new function, revamp an organization, or act as a turnaround manager for a company or department. If this sounds like you, you're likely to prefer building and moving on versus maintaining a certain function for even a short period of time.

As you read through these motivators, you may find yourself drawn to several of the items on the list—this is perfectly natural given that we humans are often a complex mix of desires, thoughts, feelings, attitudes, and beliefs.

But it's also likely that one or two of these motivators resonate as the primary motivational factors for you. By understanding what motivates you at your core, you will be better able to know which parts to hold onto and which parts you should delegate to others who may be motivated more by those activities or tasks.

Get clear now on what motivates you most, so that you can reward others later with responsibilities that align best to their own key motivations. If you do it right, you'll end up with a team with whom you will do the work that you love most, while the people who report to you will be doing the work they love most, as well. That's a win-win situation for everyone, a situation that you can provide by simply knowing your personal motivations.

Consciously Choose Your Style

Now that you have had an opportunity to think about your values and what motivates you as a manager, it is highly likely that you probably want to make some changes so that the manager you are tomorrow is highly effective and successful.

Understanding where you are and where you want to go is critical to your success. The difference between these two versions of yourself can be found in what we call the "Today-Tomorrow Gap."

Be prepared to critically analyze yourself and use the results of that analysis to define a plan that will help you to become the best manager anyone has ever worked with—ever. It will be a wild ride, so hang on!

Let's get right to it and develop that plan. This next exercise is to help you determine the type of manager you are today and the type of manager you want to be tomorrow.

First, open up an Excel worksheet on your home computer and develop the grid we've outlined below. Or, go old school and get a sheet of paper, draw a table that looks like the following diagram: (Feel free to just write in the book, too.)

Item	*Current State*	*Ideal State*	*What I Need to Do Differently*
Manager Type			
Managerial Values			
Motivation			

Now it's time to populate this chart with information that will ultimately reveal your plan for tomorrow in the final column.

For example, in an earlier exercise, if you identified yourself as a Bully rather than a Communicator, boldly write "Bully" in the "current state" box for your manager type. Then, in the "ideal state" box, write the type of manager that you would ideally seek to become. Finally, based on the characteristics of your current management state versus your ideal state, write the behavioral changes needed for you to bridge the gap so that you can become the manager you want to be for yourself and your team. Continue this exercise for your Managerial Values and Motivation based on what you learned about yourself earlier in this chapter. By pulling these components of your style together into one plan, you will be well on your way to implementing a new you, the best manager anyone has ever had—ever!

Sample Today-Tomorrow Gap Exercise

Item	*Today*	*Tomorrow*	*Bridge the Gap By:*
Manager type	Bully	Communicator	Meet regularly to update my team on programs, projects, and policies. Invite input from my team and collaboration more frequently. Find new ways for the team to proactively express their needs, skills, and ability to work together
Managerial values	Ambition Discretion Making a difference	Commitment Teamwork Effectiveness	Be more committed to the success of my team Value teamwork over my personal contributions Commit to being an effective manager

Motivation	Desire for power and fame	Love	Come from a place of support for the work that my team does, rather than focus on my own success first

Truth be told, you may exhibit characteristics of more than one managerial type today and may want to develop characteristics of more than one managerial type in the future.

What's most important about this exercise is to document where you are today and where you want to be tomorrow, and the behaviors that you need to demonstrate in order to get there.

Once you've completed this chart, you'll have created your "Today-Tomorrow Gap" analysis. Review it each and every day until you fully implement the behaviors you need to increase your effectiveness as a manager.

The "Today-Tomorrow Gap" analysis is your map to becoming the manager you know you can be. It is the first step on your journey toward learning a lot about yourself as a manager. So, get very good right now at being very clear about where you are today and where you hope to be tomorrow. After all, it is your journey—a journey that you create, along with the right map in hand.

Perfect Your Approach with Focused Learning

You have had a chance to learn about the different types of managers that exist, personal and managerial values, and various types of motivations. It is now important to take a step back and begin thinking about how you will learn to become effective manager, one who builds effective employee relationships.

While reading books like this play an important part in your process, you will learn to be a manager through having on-the-job experiences, finding a successful manager who is willing to be a mentor for you, and attending classroom training. All of these experiences are important and valuable to you as you accumulate managerial knowledge.

Mentors

Arguably one of the very best ways to become an effective manager is to learn from the mistakes of others and apply their experiences to your development. Your mentor can be your own personal "secret sauce," since absolutely no one needs to know that you have a mentor or are being coached by someone who has become successful in their own managerial right.

Identifying those people who can serve as mentors is often pretty simple. Your selection of a mentor will make or break your success, so choose wisely. A mentor can be someone who works at the same company as you, someone whose managerial success you admire, someone who holds the type of position that you seek to hold in the future, or someone who works professionally as a management coach. The important task is to choose someone who can be the right mentor for you.

The mentor you choose today may not be the mentor that you need tomorrow. And, as you grow as a manager, you may find that you turn to several different mentors to help you with different aspects of management.

That said, as a new manager, the most self-serving step you can take is to choose a mentor who can help you understand the importance of clearly seeing yourself and how your own personal experiences can be used to fuel your abilities as a manager.

To figure out who will be the right mentor for you, first list all of those people you have known professionally who could be helpful as a mentor. Then, to narrow that list down and identify the top candidates for this honored position, ask yourself these questions:

- Based on my "Today-Tomorrow Gap" analysis, what key characteristics should my mentor possess to help me narrow my skills gap?
- Of the mentors that I identified, which have the same characteristics as the person I go to when I need personal advice?
- Which potential mentor do I believe will give me open, honest, and straightforward feedback?
- Which of these potential mentors have mentored successful managers in the past?
- Have any of these individuals expressed an interest in mentoring me in the past?
- Who has the time to commit to me as a mentor?
- If I had my way, which candidate on the list would be my first, second, and third choice as a mentor? Why?

Based on your answers to these questions, identify your ideal mentor and put the wheels in motion to engage him or her as your guide to becoming a good manager. Yup, it's that simple. All you have to do is start at the top of your list and ask that candidate who's in the number one slot to be your mentor. If he or she agrees, then you can move into a formal mentoring relationship. However, if that person isn't available or doesn't feel comfortable in the role, then you can kindly thank him or her for considering the request and simply move on to the next person on the list. Soon enough, you will find a qualified person who is available and has the right type of skills to help you become an exceptional manager.

After you have identified your mentor, it is time to share with him or her some of the work that you have already been doing on your journey. Schedule time to talk about the type of manager you are today, your managerial values, and your motivations. Be sure to share your "Today-Tomorrow Gap" analysis with them. Talk to your mentor about the type of manager that you hope to become and describe the difference between your Today and Tomorrow, as you see it. From there, the two of you can discuss in depth how mentoring can help you grow into the manager you are committed to becoming.

While the specific subjects that you talk to your mentor about may change over time, what you are trying to achieve in this segment of your managerial journey should not change. At this point, you have specific behaviors that you want implement and your mentor should be helping you continually refocus your thinking on those behaviors so that you can achieve your goal. Always go back to your "Today-Tomorrow Gap" analysis as your map to what you expect to achieve and have discussions with your mentor that will help you to do just that.

A good mentor will also share with you his or her struggles, experiences, and the advice of other mentors that helped your mentor achieve the type of managerial success that he or she personally enjoys today. Learn from this person's stories. Take in all of the information your mentor shares with you and apply that knowledge to similar experiences that you are having. Most managers go through strikingly similar challenges, so listen closely. More importantly, apply the solutions that helped the mentor move through those difficult times in a way that will help you to either overcome the obstacles you're experiencing or avoid similar pitfalls altogether.

Above all else, never be defensive with your mentor. Always come from a place of compassion, love, and understanding. You chose this person to help you expand your skills and possibilities, so let your mentor do the job you have agreed to without getting in the way. If you work with a mentor successfully, you will be able to accelerate your journey and become your ideal manager of tomorrow.

Formal Training

Another way to learn how to become a manager is to attend training offered by your company.

Unfortunately, today most companies don't train their managers to build effective employee relationships. Instead, they focus most of their training time and attention on the ins and outs of functional skill development rather than helping managers to understand themselves as human beings first and taskmasters second.

If you're in a typical management training program, your company will try to train you first in your responsibilities as a functional leader of the business, a financial steward of the company, and only lastly as a manager of people.

Although these priorities are reversed, in our opinion, the training that you receive during these sessions can be exceedingly helpful, especially if you are not well-versed in project management, understanding finances, or developing strategic goals for your team. You can get a great deal of knowledge from the facilitators of these sessions, most of whom are typically not employees of your organization. As a result, you'll have the opportunity to ask the facilitator the type of hard-hitting questions you need answered so that you can do a better job with your people, rather than just focusing on the function or the finances that come along with your managerial responsibilities.

It is vitally important that you attend these training sessions. More often than not, they're developed in partnership with your company's leadership and employee development team, along with the consulting firm that was hired to design the training program. When your company offers you training to help you succeed, they're also setting the expectations they have for you as a manager. If you find this training to be a complete waste of time, offer that feedback in a way that is professional and constructive at the end of the session. Just like you are working to become a better manager, these training sessions are continuously being improved to better meet the needs of the managers with whom you work.

Learning on the Job

If your company does not offer formal manager training, don't worry. The majority of what you will learn in your pursuit to be an effective manager you will learn on the job.

It has been said that experience means you've made more mistakes, and that's certainly true when it comes to learning how to achieve excellence as a manager of people. Each day, you are going to make mistakes, screw up, and occasionally flat out fail. That is not just normal for managers, it is entirely expected. Simply put, good management is a learning process and it's what you do with your on-the-job training that provides firsthand experience.

Most people move through life repeating the same mistakes over and over again. It is common to watch managers, even those managers who say that they want to improve their skills, never make forward progress because of their chronic same-mistake syndrome. The hard part of all of this is to first recognize the mistakes that we made and then to build a plan to correct and learn from them.

For example, let's say that each time you are in a one-on-one meeting with a member of your team, that person responds by crying because he or she messed up... again. Over and over, the employee promises to work on improving performance. Then you feel badly, because an employee is crying, and subsequently you excuse his or her poor performance. Afterward, you find yourself getting angry at the fact that not only did the person perform poorly, he or she also put you through an emotional roller coaster!

Arguably, there are two problems with this scenario. The first is that you have an employee who is not adequately performing the functions of his or her role and is very good at emotional manipulation. The second problem is failing as a manager whose job is to help this person achieve the type of performance that is expected of them. So what would you do to change this scenario? Would you give up the one-on-one meetings? Preferably not. Would you have someone else in the room with you so that you are able to maintain the emotional balance? That's an option, but it could create bigger problems. Would any option work? Even though none of these options may end up being the right solution for this situation, you'll never be able to figure out what *does* work if you're not willing to try different approaches until you succeed.

Once you've learned that a given solution is not the right one to use for particular situation, *stop using it and try something else.* If that sounds like commonsense advice, it is. That's what we call on-the-job training. You experience a problem, apply a solution, and learn from the result. In those situations where the result is outstanding, multiply that solution across every similar situation. In those situations where the result is terrible, stop using that solution. It's like this: If you hit yourself in the head with a hammer and it hurt, would you hit yourself in the head with a hammer again? We certainly hope not!

So consider on-the-job training to be all about the experiences that you accumulate under your managerial belt. When you have success, do more of that. When you have failure, avoid repeating that behavior. And even if something is difficult and doesn't feel right, if it has an exceptionally good outcome, continue doing it. Sometimes the hardest things to do are the most important to get done.

As a manager, you should pause and frequently reflect on your experiences with the people that you are responsible for managing. Create a file for each member of your team, and continually update it with examples of managerial behavior that works well for that person, as well a list of those behaviors that seem to get the exact opposite result that you seek.

Over time, you'll be able to amass a great deal of information about how you can behave as a manager to get the right type of responses from each member of your team. But, you'll only be able to do this if you remain exceptionally conscious about the outcomes of the tactics that you employ as a manager. Observe and record your successes and failures over time.

If you track your on-the-job training exceptionally well, your team members will soon begin to realize that you have an in depth knowledge of who they are and a full understanding of their contributions to your team's collective success. Demonstrating that you understand your employees as human beings will propel your ability to build effective and long-lasting relationships. When you consistently apply the right solutions and behaviors, you will be amazed at how little time you will need to spend with hands-on management. You'll start to see better results than you've ever had before and your team will respond with higher performance.

But most importantly, this management tactic will help you understand the specific strengths of individual members of your team and help you understand how best to motivate them to give their very best.

Ask for Help Before You Need It

Even with the deepest understanding of oneself, the very simple fact is that no one succeeds alone; but when people fail, it is because they failed alone without asking for help.

As a manager, perhaps the most important managerial tools you could ever have are the wisdom, experience, and training of others. The people around you all have a wealth of information and knowledge, so when you need help, ask for it. There will always be someone there and available to share their knowledge with you.

Nothing about management is new, mostly because human beings have been managing other human beings since nearly the dawn of time. As a result, there is a huge amount of information, tactics, and training available to help you succeed in the very important role of helping others to succeed in support of your company's specific and stated strategy.

Even in those situations where you feel you already have the right answer to solve a specific problem, there can be no harm in running your solution past a manager, mentor, or the members of your team. Being there for you is part of their job; just as your job is to help them succeed, as well.

You don't have to take advice from anyone; but by asking for input, you might just see the situation that you're dealing with a little bit differently.

If you're the kind of manager who finds it impossible to ask for help, you should immediately consider a new line of work. If you take nothing else away from this entire book, take away the fact that *you will need help and you will need to ask for it*. Ric Ocasek, lead singer of the Cars, was quoted saying, "Refusing to ask for help when you need it is refusing someone the chance to be helpful." (Quotes) You wouldn't want to let others down by not offering an opportunity to be helpful would you? When you ask for help, your humanity shines right through. Others respond exceptionally well to humanity. What they don't respond well to is a "know-it-all." So, ask for help and get comfortable with receiving what you ask for.

To prove to you that asking for help is a win-win solution, go ahead and put this book down right now and ask the first person you see for help with something—anything! Go on now. Give it a try. You can always pick up this book again once you have established the fact that you can ask for and accept help in whatever form it is offered.

Those who ask for help are the same people who are willing to learn, who know their limitations, and who want to grow their ability to be an exceptional manager.

Express Yourself Responsibly

When it comes to being an excellent manager, the emotions you bring with you are important to evaluate and address. This includes the emotional baggage you have collected over the years just by being human—this baggage can manifest in your day-to-day existence at work and can inform you on how well you manage people.

Contrary to popular wisdom, there is a place for emotions in your professional life and in the workplace. As a matter of fact, the emotions you and your colleagues bring to your job responsibilities can help you make or break a company. Some of the best CEOs in the world actively and vocally express their passion for the work their organization does through exceedingly emotional speeches, press conferences, and employee meetings. Of course, we mostly see this kind of emotional display only when things are going very well for the company; CEOs are rarely seen crying about the state of their business when things aren't going all that well, or when they're in the limelight for something they've done terribly wrong.

It is safe to say that having a good grasp on your emotional state, knowing when and how your emotions are going to be useful, and understanding the purpose of emotions in the workplace can lead you to exceptional success as a manager. After all, every single member of your team has emotions, too. Emotions are what connect us as human beings and serve as an anchor in the creation of effective employee relationships.

One of your first jobs as a manager is to understand your own personal emotional state. To do this, you will want to examine how you react emotionally to specific scenarios, and how you present those emotions to your team. It is through your own personal emotional responses to various scenarios that you will be better able to help your team manage their emotional reactions. In addition, it is through your emotional responses to these scenarios that your team will truly understand who you are as a human being and be better able to connect with you as a good manager or label you a bad boss.

These simple emotional connections can make or break you, because they form the basis of your team's trust in you as a manager. People trust people who they believe to be authentic. When you are authentic, you express your emotions honestly. Some companies will ask you to leave your emotions at the door—don't do it! If you divorce yourself from your emotions, your team may believe that you do not care about the things that are important to them because you don't react to a given situation in a way that reflects their emotional involvement. If your team thinks you don't care about them or their issues, then your team will not care about you. And it is through this lack of emotion that the relationship between manager and employee degrades.

Human emotion is a huge field of study, and in these pages we can't begin to encompass the range of research done. But there are a few studies that should be helpful to you in your journey to understand your emotional responses in the workplace.

While the continuum of human emotion is much broader, in 2001, W. Gerrod Parrott, a professor at Georgetown University, defined the six basic emotions as: love, joy, surprise, anger, sadness, and fear. (Parrott)

Six Basic Emotions	
Love	Tender affection for somebody, such as a close relative or friend, or for something, such as a place, an ideal, or an animal.
Joy	Feelings of great happiness or pleasure, especially of an elevated or spiritual kind.
Surprise	Sudden wonder or amazement, especially at something unexpected.
Anger	A strong feeling of grievance and displeasure.
Sadness	The feeling of grief or sorrow.
Fear	An unpleasant feeling of anxiety or apprehension caused by the presence or anticipation of danger.

Emotions are powerful. You feel them. You express them. You use them to inspire your team, express the urgency of a situation, and more. No one can tell you what your emotional state must be at any given moment of any given day. And no one can take your emotions away from you or tell you how to feel. But again, your emotions can make or break your function, your team's success, or the relationship you have with your employees.

As a result, you have a great deal of responsibility as a manager to appropriately apply your emotions effectively and consciously in the workplace. You and only you are responsible for your emotional state.

While it is true that certain behaviors and situations would spark a similar emotional response in most people, no one on your team is responsible for how you feel.

And those managers who understand and take full responsibility for their emotional state tend to succeed to a far greater degree than those managers who aren't able to achieve that kind of insight and control. Why? Because people respect others who are able to recognize their own emotional reactions without assigning blame to others for their individual response.

As such, the best advice a manager can get from any mentor anywhere in the world is to spend time getting to know yourself emotionally. Figure out just exactly why you tend to express love toward one employee and disdain toward another. Document all of the ways that your experience as a manager brings you joy. Examine why you do or do not like surprises. Determine why sadness creeps up at certain times of the week, month, or year. And finally, get to know your hot buttons—those situations or scenarios that make your head explode with anger.

Understand Your Emotional Dark Side

Emotional baggage contains negative and unresolved issues that can creep into your work place and suck the creativity and innovative thinking out of anyone. In your role as a manager, you're solving problems right and left, day after day, month after month; you're a nonstop solution factory. And while that last sentence may seem a bit melodramatic, the drama that it implies is meant to reflect the critically important role that creativity and innovation play in any manager's life.

According to Parrott, half of all emotions that are available to you as core emotions are on the negative side of the emotional spectrum. Stop to think about that model for a second. If half of all emotions are negative, then you have a great deal of work to do to ensure that you are appropriately letting go of negativity so that you can properly progress as a manager.

Negative Emotions	
Anger	A strong feeling of grievance and displeasure.
Sadness	The feeling of grief or sorrow.
Fear	An unpleasant feeling of anxiety or apprehension caused by the presence or anticipation of danger.

Now, let's start by delving a bit deeper into each one of these emotions and examining how they may play out for you as a manager.

Anger

Have you ever just gotten really mad? We're not talking about a little bit upset because someone cuts you off as you're driving to work: we are talking about completely seeing "red." If you're anything like the rest of us, you've experienced the type of anger we are talking about.

For most, anger pops up when we feel that we or someone or something we care about has been mistreated, disrespected, unfairly categorized, or unjustly attacked. As one of the core negative emotions, this one is exceedingly important for you to understand as a manager. Left unchecked and unmanaged, anger can lead to violence. And while violence is never acceptable in the workplace, let alone anywhere else, it is exceedingly important for you to ensure that you have your own personal anger under control.

Humans get angry. It's natural. And if anger is one of the negative emotions that you are carrying around with you, it is your responsibility to know how to effectively manage it within your managerial duties, to the benefit of the people around you.

And while anger is categorized here as a negative emotion, it is appropriate to point out that getting mad at someone and expressing that anger in a productive way can and often is an acceptable, appropriate part of a working relationship. In other words, it is ok to get angry, as long as that anger is not acted on in an irrational, destructive manner. Expressing your anger constructively is a good way to show your employees that you are in fact an emotional human being.

You need to be able to recognize when you're feeling angry, know exactly what incites anger within you, and have an ironclad grasp on the signs that your anger may be getting out of control. While there is also some merit in negative emotions, when used wisely, we will touch on it later in this chapter.

Sadness

Sadness comes in many shapes and sizes. It is one of the negative emotions that can be easily misunderstood. Often, when an employee hears that an expectation was not met, he or she will identify their response as sadness. As a human, you may even tell your team that the fact that they did not hit their performance measures saddens you. But are you really sad? Is your employee? Most likely, the emotional state that you experience when a team member does not hit the mark is probably more closely related to disappointment, the first cousin of sadness.

As a manager, your team will be able to tell when you are genuinely happy and sad, and everything in between. Humans can easily pick up on the emotions of others; and with sadness comes a lot of sympathy. Think of it, when you encounter a friend who has just been fired from a job, you tend to feel sorry for the person. Likewise, when you struggle over and over again to accomplish something that is for the good of your company, but you just can't get support, you may grieve for the organization, which can feel very much like sadness.

Understanding what sadness feels like is an important step in building effective employee relationships because being emotionally authentic builds trust! What is critically important when it comes to sadness is to first understand where it comes from. If you struggle with sadness, spend time thinking about why the issue is popping up. If you can't come to a conclusion as to why you are struggling with sadness.

Fear

If there is one emotion that everyone would agree is common to the workplace, it's fear—fear of not getting promoted, fear of not getting a raise, fear of not being accepted, fear of not getting along, and probably most commonly, fear of getting fired. Fear is the enemy of building effective relationships.

As a manager, you can conquer fear. But to do so, you have to figure out why you are afraid. Fear tends to stem entirely from the interpersonal relationships we have with others.

Whether you realize it or not, fear is very closely related to trust. When you trust in the fact that you are doing the best job that you can do and that it will be rewarded, fear of not being promoted doesn't have space to breathe. Similarly, when you trust that you have enough money in the bank to live for a certain amount of time, the fear of getting fired— more specifically, the fear of not being able to pay your living expenses—starts to disappear.

One way to approach a thorough understanding of what causes you to feel fear is to deeply examine the feeling.

In nearly every white-collar crime drama, the hero detective is inevitably instructed to "follow the money." The process is just as successful when you're trying to uncover the source of your fear. If you "follow the fear" all the way to the root, you'll discover the absence of love that is the source of the feeling.

President Franklin D. Roosevelt's famous quote, "The only thing we have to fear is fear itself," is still relevant today. But what he didn't say is that when you let go of fear, you will indeed live a life that is happier, healthier, and more productive; a life that brings far more positive experiences to the people around you.

Fear Destroys Accomplishment

Negative emotions can weigh you down and get in the way of your success, not just as a manager, but in every facet of your life. So it's important to understand how you participate with negative emotions, identify those triggers that allow you to react negatively, and make a plan to move forward in a way that is healthy not just for you but for the members of your team.

As described earlier in this book, we have six basic emotions. These emotions sit on a continuum from positive to negative. You can think of this emotional continuum as two sides of the same coin. On the positive side, you'll find love, joy, and surprise. On the opposite side of the coin, you have anger, sadness, and fear. However, for most of us, it is far easier to understand the emotional range from a linear point of view. As a matter of fact, since the six emotions we have identified above are considered core emotions, there are hundreds of emotions—some yet to be accurately identified—that connect one core motion to the next.

The two emotional pillars are love and fear. The remaining emotions—joy, surprise, anger, and sadness—are the emotions that connect the two pillars. So, when you experience joy and surprise (as well as all the emotions in between), then you are in essence experiencing positive emotions associated with love.

Conversely, when you experience anger and sadness, and all of the emotions that connect the negative range of feelings, then essentially you are experiencing fear. And it's important to note that fear can kill you!

In all seriousness, it isn't money that is the root of all evil, it's fear. While fear is the exact opposite of love, it is similar to love in the sense that there is a great deal of passion, dedication, and commitment when an individual experiences fear.

So, to understand which negative emotions are weighing you down, first confront fear and understand your own personal commitment and dedication to that emotion.

To help you get to a clear understanding of your personal relationship with fear, we've developed a list of questions meant to help you reflect on your experience with fear, as well as understand why it pops up in your life, how you react to it, and, which negative emotions you may be experiencing that are rooted in fear. There are 15 questions, which might feel like a lot to answer, but just take them one at a time. In your pursuit to be a good manager, it is well worth spending time on this exercise; the questions should take at least 30 minutes and no more than one hour. Clearly, since you are looking for insight, this isn't something you should rush through. Answer as honestly as you can.

You will find that not all of the questions deal directly with your role as a manager. That's entirely by design. It's important to your success that you, as a human being in the position to manage others, clearly know who you are in this world, as a member of your family, as a manager at your company, and as the leader of a team.

But before you spend time answering the questions below, sit quietly, breathe deeply, and clear your mind. When you consider these questions, think rationally. Some of these questions will resonate with you, while others may leave you scratching your head and wondering what they may have to do with you or your life. That's perfectly natural. The goal here is to have you document the negative feelings that you encounter as you move through your day from morning to night.

Negative Emotions Questionnaire	
When you wake up in the morning, what is the first thing you think of?	
How do you feel as you start your day?	
When you are en route to your place of employment, what crosses your mind?	
As you sit in the first meeting of the day, are you fully engaged in what is happening or does your mind wander?	
Do you feel that your peers are collaborative?	
Do you take a lunch break?	
When you do take a lunch break, do you get out of the office and have a social interaction with	

other employees?	
When your boss asks for something to be done, do you immediately jump on it and speed to finish the project so that his or her expectations are met?	
Are there bullies at work? How do they make you feel?	
Are you satisfied with your career progression?	
Do you have work-life balance?	
Are you able to get all of your work done during normal working hours?	
When you get home in the evening, are you exhausted?	
In the evening, do you attend social events with friends or have time to spend with your family?	
When you prepare for bed, do you easily fall asleep or does your mind start racing?	

If your answers indicate that your day is more or less consumed with negative feelings, repeat this exercise for an entire week. By repeating this exercise for an entire week, you will be able to determine if there are particular patters that become apparent to you. You may find that you are just upset in the mornings and by mid-day you are fine...that probably just means you are tired. However, you might find that you are upset for most of the day and that your feelings are centered on a particular negative emotion. In that case, you can build a plan to resolve the issue that is causing this fear-based emotion. However, you might just find that you had a bad day and that most of your days are filled with love.

Conversely, if you find that you rarely encounter negative emotions, consider diving a little deeper into your day, because every one of us experiences negativity in one way or another on a daily basis. If you do not recognize it, you may be in a state of denial, which indicates an entirely different psychological state, for which a professional may be able to help.

It is our job in getting to know ourselves through this exercise to be upfront and honest, which will help you to be upfront and honest with our employees in the long run.

Stop the Behaviors that Don't Serve You

Now that you have spent some time contemplating your relationship with those emotions on the fear side of the emotional continuum, it is time to stop using the negative emotions that no longer serve you.

Negative emotions not only get in the way of living a happy and healthy life, they spill out into the workplace and have a negative impact on the work you produce, as well as your team relationships.

Based on your responses to the questionnaire, the next step is for you to begin to identify trend emotions—those emotions that tend to be with you most of the time. Because these are your own emotions, this next step will be a lot easier than you imagine. However, it's much harder to help a colleague, friend, or partner through this exercise because you do not have the exact insight into another person's emotional experiences.

So let's get to it. Identify the negative emotion you use most frequently.

If you're one of those "check your e-mail before you get out of bed" people, what's your motivation for behaving this way? Are you angry that you have to do your job? Probably not. Do you feel a great deal of sadness about the e-mail that came in and what you have to do to get the work done that day? Unlikely.

What's more likely is that—either consciously or subconsciously—you genuinely love the fact that you play a significant role in your company, so significant that you must immediately respond to e-mail each and every morning, even before you start your morning rituals.

Or, on the other end of the emotional continuum, you fear your boss's reaction if you do not immediately respond to e-mail. Of course this is just one example of how to get to the core emotion you are feeling, and you can see how the negative emotion you are experiencing may actually stem from the positive side of the emotional continuum.

Continuing on with the negative emotional deduction, your job now is to figure out why fear plays a part in your life. To do just that, dig deep into some of the secondary emotions that may be popping up for you along the fear side of the continuum. It's important to look deep into the core emotions that may be getting in your way. Document all of this for yourself so that as you progress, you can look back for clues to your emotional commitments.

Anger

Anger is very similar to surprise. That's why so many people claim to dislike surprises, because it is such a similar feeling within our human psyche as anger. So, if anger is popping up as the core negative emotion that you deal with most, it is likely that you dislike being surprised and want to be able to control every situation that you are in.

Being out of control is likely the most important secondary emotion that you should deal with. It sits between surprise and anger. So then the question that you have to answer for yourself is this: Why do I always need to be in control?

What is it about yourself that craves being in charge? Were you not in control growing up? Or, maybe you're not in control of the rest of your life and being in control at work is your way of finding balance. Whatever the case may be, looking deeply into your need for control is the most important thing you can do if you are commonly responding with anger.

Now, as a manager, think about how anger affects your team. If your team messes up, they may not tell you if you respond in anger. As a matter of fact, if anger is your "go to" response, you will only hear positive reports of success from your team. Then, when something blows up, it is likely that your team will try to manage through the process without you, which will hurt your career in the long run and diminish your ability to facilitate effective employee relationships. If anger gets in your way, identify it now and start the process of leaving this emotional baggage behind.

Sadness

Sadness is the negative emotion that sits between anger and fear. Sadness sits right in the middle and often causes emotional confusion for the person who is experiencing it. Sadness doesn't have the passion of anger or the intensity of fear. However, if sadness is popping up for you as the core negative emotion that you are dealing with most frequently, it is likely that you are dealing with a control issue, too.

The control issue manifests differently in the case of sadness then the one resulting from anger. You probably do not have a great deal of need to be in control of any given situation: however, it is highly likely that you experience negativity as something that happened to you, essentially being a victim of the situation. Victimization or feeling like a victim is exceedingly common in all cultures. This is nothing to be ashamed of, at all. Sadness washes over us when we experience a loss, something that is entirely out of our control, such as the death of a loved one. In the workplace, sadness typically indicates that you've given up, are just doing the work with no motivation to excel, and are devoid of any hope that your workplace will get better.

As a manager, your sadness will affect your team in an entirely different way. It can result in a number of reactions; but probably the most common reaction you will get from your team is pity. They will likely feel sorry for you. They may even start to avoid you because being with you diminishes their own positivity. And while sadness has its place and is a normal human reaction to loss, it can be a destructive force as well. If you experience a great deal of sadness, get to the root of the issue right away and start to change your outlook on life so that you can succeed if you decided that management is the right place for you.

Fear

As the source of all negative emotions, fear is present in both sadness and anger.

Fear usually stems from the unknown. For example, when you watch a very scary movie and the main character is walking down the rickety wooden stairs into a stone basement, and that action is coupled with dim lighting and freaky music, it is easy to become afraid of what is going to happen. Conversely, when you watch the same scene with the sound off, your sense of fear is likely to be greatly diminished. So, whenever possible, take time to get rid of external influences that lead to you believe something is scary—such as the creepy music in a scary movie—and focus on what you are dealing with… just walking down unsafe stairs.

Fear also has a connection to a lack of control. In this case, you just don't know what's going to happen, and by not knowing what's coming next, fear of the unknown invades your life.

In a professional situation, the fear that most people experience is the fear of being fired. However, when you look at the actual statistics, being fired is a rare occurrence. It is much more common to see people quit their jobs.

So why would fear erupt as such a dominant emotion in the workplace? It's simple. Each of us wants to have security, to feel that no matter what happens we will be able to take care of ourselves and our family, and continue to lead the life we know.

As a manager, if you are going to work every day in fear of what is going to happen next, you are giving fear a leading role in the way that you manage your team. As a result, it's highly likely that your team will not trust you. Rather, they will probably fear you, since that is the emotion you are projecting unconsciously. If they fear you, they will not talk to you, have a relationship with you, or work collaboratively toward increasing productivity.

You may be surprised to learn that there's some good news here even for those of us who operate principally from a place of fear. The good news is that fear is the exact opposite of love and these two emotions are strikingly similar, which is a somewhat controversial view that is covered in the next section. So if you are experiencing fear as your primary negative emotion, get to the bottom of what you are afraid of —fast! Fear is like a tumor. You might not see it at first, but it can grow very quickly and kill your career.

By now, you should have a pretty clear view of which core negative emotion you are dealing with most frequently. The next step is to address these emotions and focus on letting go of control.

Releasing your commitment to a negative emotion is a process. It takes time and doesn't happen overnight. Concentrate not just on letting go of what you are trying to control when the negative emotion pops up, but also on retraining your brain to think differently.

To get you started, create a list of up to 10 affirmations that you want in your day-to-day life. Affirmations are positive statements, and these statements will move you from negativity to positivity, setting the stage for a happy, healthy, and productive lifestyle. You should have no more than 10 affirmations on your list. Any more than that will dilute the impact of this exercise.

Example Affirmations

1. I live a comfortable life full of love and support.
2. I'm aware and in control of my emotional reactions and have exceptionally mature relationships with others.
3. I am confident.
4. I have the right people in place to help me successfully run my department.
5. I am surrounded by friends who help me succeed each and every day.
6. I love and use my intense kindness to create exceptionally productive workplaces for my team.
7. I give myself permission to experience joy each and every day.
8. I am patient and kind and people sincerely like me.
9. I have a close loving relationship with my partner, which is built upon mutual love and respect.
10. Love is the core of my emotional being.

Once you have your list perfected, speak your list out loud each day. You do not need an audience for this exercise, but when you put this practice into your daily ritual, you will soon be able to move away from the negative emotions that you experience and toward positive emotions that can help you live more successfully. This practice is firmly rooted in the Law of Attraction. Simply put, what you ask for, concentrate on, and work toward will manifest in your life. There are a number of books on the market that can help you to understand the Law of Attraction far better than we would be able to do it justice here.

By using those emotions that are on the side of love, you will be able to produce amazing results, both on your own and with your team. These positive emotions will help everyone that you manage or come in contact with at work want to work hard for you when you need it. You'll even get to go home feeling that you have accomplished something important and meaningful during the day, which can be celebrated with your family at night.

Now that you have spent a great deal of time getting to know yourself and where your negative emotions come from, it is critically important to not go too far in the eradication of your fear. After all, you are a human being. You experience a wide range of emotions. Experiencing fear is a natural emotional warning sign that something is wrong.

Perfect Isn't Perfection

One of the deepest pitfalls managers can descend into is a feeling or expectation that you have to be perfect. Managers, especially those who are a little light on experience, put a great deal of pressure on themselves. They tend to believe that they have to be perfect because other people are looking up to them, that their skill set has to be better than everyone around them, that they have to be more engaging than even their own bosses, that they can never make a mistake, etcetera, etcetera, etcetera. The worst part is, in reaction to all this self-imposed pressure, managers can often come off as a bit robotic or impersonal, resulting in the development of less than optimal employee relationships.

The truth is that even the best managers make mistakes. In fact, one common attribute that all good managers share is that they let their humanity shine through. When they have a negative emotional response to a given situation, they own it. They never blame someone else for their reaction. Some even take a great deal of pride in the fact that they only have one or two triggers that fuel an intense reaction. Many times employees will recognize a manager's emotional maturity and seek opportunities to join his or her team.

To ensure that you are seen as an approachable, caring, and ultimately sincere manager, you may choose to retain one of your negative emotional reactions—as long as you learn how to manage it productively. Consciously decide upon the negative emotional reaction that will serve you best in the workplace and in your role as a manager. Don't let the emotional reaction choose you.

In some cases, negative emotions can be used as a motivating force to get work done. The goal, however, is to use negative emotions sparingly. Remember, overusing negative emotions will not bring people closer to you; rather, negative emotions will push people further and further away, which will cripple your ability to be an effective manager of people.

For example, if you are a manager who is responsible for the financial picture of your company, it would be common for you to react negatively to mistakes made in the accounting process. Your desire for quality and the work that your team produces naturally would be a great place for you to apply your emotional self, both positively and negatively. However, your negative emotional reaction to the color of ink an employee uses to fill in a text box wouldn't be aligned to the proper use of your negative emotional tool. In other words, don't sweat the small stuff.

Conversely, if you are a creative director responsible for the look and feel of a brand, the misuse of color would be an important place to apply a negative emotional response so that your team understands the value you place on quality design. In this case, it is important to sweat the small stuff.

The point here is this: Your employees need to be able to predict how you, as their manager, will react to any given situation. There is a time and a place to apply negativity. However, you will not be an effective manager if you apply a negative emotional response to every situation that does not meet your fancy. So, choose now what behavior will elicit a negative emotional response from you. Then, commit to yourself that you will choose to discuss other issues without allowing negative emotions into the conversation. You are taking on a great deal of responsibility in managing others, and your ability to manage will depend greatly on recognizing that your emotional state plays a significant role in the success of your team. It is your emotions that will fuel the development of effective employee relationships.

Double Down on the Power of Positivity

If you're anything like the rest of us, you have a great deal of positive emotions to apply toward the development of effective employee relationships. The good news is that positive emotions can be an awesome tool to use with your employees, because positive emotions can fuel creativity and innovative thinking. All of which are great building blocks for relationships.

In your role as a manager, you're tasked with solving problems every day, removing obstacles blocking your team's success, and getting through your company's biggest challenges. When you approach all of this from a state of positivity, you are empowered to overcome every challenge, every time.

You should think of the positive emotions that you experience as the rocket fuel that helps a jet to take off. Not only can this fuel get an enormous jet from the gate to the end of the runway, it can propel the jet into the sky with what feels like minimal effort.

But staying positive—and avoiding the easy rut we can slip into with negativity—can take a lot effort. Positivity requires focus, strength, commitment, and a heck of a lot of energy.

Just like a jet taking off into the sky, you choose to be one of those managers that your employees will remember for the rest of their lives, and for all of the right reasons. You can decide from your first day in your role as manager that the careers of your employees are as important as yours. Fuel their success by giving them encouragement, helpful ideas, and the type of influence they need to get their ideas into the executive suite.

As we outlined earlier, Parrott defined six core emotions, three of which sit on the positive side of the emotional continuum. According to his model, half of all emotions that are available to you as core emotions are positive. Positive? That's right. Positive. Half of all of the emotions that are available to you can help you succeed as a manager, if you apply them sincerely.

Positive Emotions	
Love	Tender affection for somebody, such as a close relative or friend, or for something, such as a place, an ideal, or an animal.
Joy	Feelings of great happiness or pleasure, especially of an elevated or spiritual kind.
Surprise	Sudden wonder or amazement, especially at something unexpected.

Those seem like pretty good emotions, right? Well, let's go a little deeper into what positive emotions can do for you.

Surprise

Some people just hate surprises, which is no surprise since surprise is right next to anger on the emotional continuum. However, those of us who love nothing more than super special surprises have a lot of great times to share with our employees.

For most, surprise pops up when we feel that someone has done something special for us—something that reflects an unexpected depth of consideration that just knocks our socks off. As a manager, surprise is one of the best emotional rewards that you can offer your employees, especially those who live on the positive side of the emotional spectrum. Why? Because when you plan a surprise for your employees, they realize that you care about them and their contributions to your team's collective success.

Joy

Joy, sitting between surprise and love, is pure happiness. It can serve you exceptionally well as a manager, because people like people who live with a great sense of joy. Think about it—doesn't everyone love to hear other people laugh and express happiness? Well, that's joy! Joy draws people to you and it keeps people coming back for more.

As a manager, you can bring joy into work with you every day. While not every situation can be a happy one, you can approach your work in general from a joyful, emotional core, which will give those people who work with you a great feeling by just being in your presence. Whether you're attending a meeting together, having a one-on-one discussion, or collaborating on a project, if you are bringing a sense of joy to your workday, you will have a profoundly positive effect on those around you.

And when the people around you feel good, you'll find you're able to get what you need more easily, more quickly, and with more and varied support. Joy is contagious. Once you catch it, it's hard to get rid of and very easy to pass along.

Love

Love is the most basic of the core emotions. It fuels all other positive emotions and is the most beautiful of all emotional situations that one can achieve. And if you think love has no place in the work world, we're here to lovingly tell that you couldn't be more wrong.

When most people think about love, they think of a lover or loved one; however, as a manager, love can be your core strength. If you have genuine appreciation for a colleague, you are likely to be more patient, kind, and respectful of that person. So it follows that if you can develop genuine affection for your team members—if you can cultivate loving feelings for each one of them—you'll be well on your way to becoming "Manager of the Year," because your team will return this love to you.

An additional bonus of learning to harness all these positive emotions is the wonderful creativity, innovation, and respect that come along with positivity. Life lived positively simply feels better!

Commitment to Good

Unlike negative emotions, which can weigh you down and get in your way, positive emotions can build you up and contribute a great deal to your success, not just in your professional life, but in your private life too.

Study after study has shown that happy people live healthier lives and are more productive. So in the same way that we did a deep dive into the source of our negative emotions in order to understand their influence on our personal and professional lives, we need to understand and identify those triggers that allow us to react positively to a given situation, and make a plan to move forward in ways that will more easily result in positive emotional responses from ourselves and those around us.

One more time for emphasis: Think back to our full discussion of how the emotional continuum moves from positive to negative? On the positive side, you find love, joy, and surprise; on the negative side you find their opposites—anger, sadness, and fear.

Most of us find it easier to understand and relate to positive emotions because positive emotions tend to help us live better lives. After all, who wouldn't want to live a life that is filled with love?

To help you get to a clear understanding of your personal relationship with love, the anchor emotion that supports the positive emotional continuum, take a moment to answer the positive emotion questionnaire below.

But before you do, remember that this list of questions is only meant to help you reflect on your experience with love, to more clearly understand why it pops up in your life and how you react to it, as well as help you identify which positive emotions you may be experiencing most frequently and why.

Just as you did before considering your negative emotional commitments, take a moment to sit quietly, breathe deeply, and clear your mind before answering these positive emotion questions. It is critically important that you are not in a highly emotional state when you consider these questions so that you can rationally identify how love plays a role in your life.

You will find that not all of the questions deal directly with your role as a manager. As a human being in the position to manage others, you must clearly know who you are—in this world, in your family, in your company, and as the leader of your team—to facilitate effective relationships with employees.

You'll notice that that these questions are almost identical to the ones you were asked to respond to when you were learning about how your negative emotions affect your work life.

The positive and negative emotion questionnaires are primarily the same because both positive and negative emotions play a role in your life. However, for this exercise you should consider how you feel from the positive perspective as you answer the below questions. You should spend not less than 30 minutes and no more than one hour on this exercise. Be very honest with yourself during this exercise and think deeply about the positive side of your experiences as you document your answers.

Positive Emotions Questionnaire	
When you wake up in the morning, what is the first thing you think of?	
How do you feel as you start your day?	
When you are en route to your place of employment, what crosses your mind?	
As you sit in the first meeting of the day, are you fully engaged in what is happening or does your mind wander?	
Do you feel that your peers are collaborative?	

Do you take a lunch break?	
When you do take a lunch break, do you get out of the office and have a social interaction with other employees?	
When your boss asks for something to be done, do you immediately jump on it and speed to finish the project so that your boss's expectations are met?	
Do you have friends at work? How do they make you feel?	
Are you satisfied with your career progression?	
Do you have work-life balance?	
Are you able to get all of your work done during normal working hours?	

When you get home in the evening, are you exhausted?	
In the evening, do you attend social events with friends or have time to spend with your family?	
When you prepare for bed, do you easily fall asleep or does your mind start racing?	

Of course, just as the rest of us do, you'll have both positive and negative feelings and reactions throughout the day. The goal here is to recognize that even in the worst of circumstances, you also have positive emotions that fuel your day.

If you find that you rarely encounter positive emotions, consider diving a little deeper into your day. It is your job to get to know yourself through this exercise and to be upfront and honest about who you are, how you react, and where positivity plays a role. The fact remains that negativity can interrupt your success; so focusing on your use of positive emotions can help you achieve success.

There may well be other questions that you ponder as a result of asking yourself these 15 positive emotion questions. If you do have other questions come up, again consider it a special gift. Not only are you consciously thinking about which positive emotions pop up for you throughout the day, but your subconscious is also bringing forward other emotions that it wants you to consciously consider as part of this process.

Turn Affirmation into Action

Okay, enough thinking, it's time for action!

At this point, you have identified the one negative emotion that you will continue to bring along with you in your life and activities as a manager of people. You are conscious of the role this negative emotion will play. You have also thought deeply about how positive emotions play a role in your day-to-day life. So, let's put it all together and create a plan through which you can responsibly use your emotions to build effective relationships in the workplace.

First, gather your answers to the list of questions when you thought about both your positive and negative emotions. For each question, determine which emotion best represents the emotional reaction you have, and then fill that box in. Example: If "sadness" is the primary emotional response that you feel when you start your day, then you would color in the sadness box on that row.

Emotional Continuum Blotter

	Love	Joy	Surprise	Anger	Sadness	Fear
When you wake up in the morning, what is the first thing you think of?						

How do you feel as you start your day?						
When you are en route to your place of employment, what crosses your mind?						
As you sit in the first meeting of the day, are you fully engaged in what is happening or does your mind wander?						
Do you feel that your peers are collaborative?						
Do you take a lunch break?						
When you do take a lunch break, do you get out of the office and						

have a social interaction with other employees?						
When your boss asks for something to be done, do you immediately jump on it and speed to finish the project so that his or her expectations are met?						
Are there bullies at work? How do they make you feel?						
Are you satisfied with your career progression?						
Do you have work-life balance?						
Are you able to get all of your work done during						

normal working hours?						
When you get home in the evening, are you exhausted?						
In the evening, do you attend social events with friends or have time to spend with your family?						
When you prepare for bed, do you easily fall asleep or does your mind start racing?						

By coloring in the boxes, you now have a visual representation of the emotions that most affect your life, as well as a numeric value, by adding together the number of shaded boxes for each emotion. Now, determine which side of the emotional continuum you spend more time in during your day. For example, if you find that you feel angry for the better part of each day—by a lot of shaded boxes—then you spend most of your time on the fear side of the proverbial emotional coin. Conversely, if you find that there is a great deal of joy in your life, then you are indeed spending more time on the love side of the equation.

The goal is to see where you spend more time, in love or in fear, and then move those of us who spend more time on the fear side toward the love side so that we can positively impact the work we do and the people around us. This movement from fear to love isn't easy; fear has a strong grip. But just like anything that you want to accomplish in this world, you need a plan. Let's call it your positivity plan!

To develop your positivity plan, you will first need to list in order of priority the negative emotions that pop up for you in your day-to-day life.

Prioritizing the negative emotion as a manager is a critical first step in this exercise. As we did in the earlier exercise, there may be negative emotions that are in some way serving you in the workplace; however, they may not be serving you in your personal life, or vice versa. To get to the prioritization of your negative emotions, consider which negative emotions are getting in your way in the workplace first, which may be very different negative emotions than those that are getting in the way of your home life.

Now, list those three core negative emotions with the negative emotion that gets in your way most frequently at the top and the one that is getting in your way the least at the bottom. If you want to make a real change in your life, you have to focus on eliminating those emotions that get in your way the most. Learn to manage that emotion first in a concentrated way, rather than trying to eliminate every negative emotion all at once.

Next, on the same piece of paper, identify the exact opposite positive emotion. So for example, if you are spending the majority of your day in anger, then you would want to list joy as the emotion that you want to move toward.

Then, start to document the difference for you personally between the negative emotion you want to eliminate and the positive emotion you want present in your life. Seems pretty difficult, doesn't it? Well, it is. But nothing worth having comes easily.

For example, to move from anger to joy, you first have to list the reasons anger frequently pops up for you. Then, on the same sheet, write the reasons that joy is present in your life. Looking at this information, you may see some commonalities; however, your job here is to determine your plan of action. How will you respond from a place of love to those behavioral points that would most commonly elicit anger?

Let's spell this out in a real-life example. Imagine being asked into a meeting by a vice president in your group. During that meeting, you tell the vice president that the issues she is describing are a result of her own behavior. She responds by standing up and screaming that she is leaving the meeting and never speaking to you ever again. As a matter of fact, she all but says you should go ahead and start packing up your desk. Well, normally in that situation, those of us who respond with anger would stand up and start screaming back. We might even go ahead and tell her she can go straight to hell.

This is where your positivity plan can be of great help. When you have a clear plan that guides you in your response to negativity, you can manage through this type of difficult situation with ease and grace. By clearly identifying why you respond to a situation with anger, and documenting how you will respond with a positive emotion can turn this terrible event around and make it life changing for you and this VP.

Having clearly documented responses to how you will manage this type of attack, practicing your responses ahead of time, and committing to a response based in the core emotion of love will help you build effective employee relationships. Your plan may include statements such as:

- When someone yells at me, I quietly sit back in my chair and remain silent until they are done screaming.

- During a hostile confrontation, I fold my hands in my lap so that my hands are touching each other. I use my hands touching each other to remind me to remain calm.

- When I am ready to respond verbally, I speak at a volume that is quieter than my normal conversation volume.

- When I am ready to respond verbally to an attack, I remained seated, speak softly, and ask the attacker for additional explanation about his or her point of view before I provide input.

- As the attacker provides more information, I use this time to gather my thoughts and prepare my response.

- As I calm my mind, listen to the attacker's point of view, I use that time to identify the one or two reasons why I respect this person or why I enjoy being around this individual.

- As I begin my response, I keep in mind that this person is emotionally on the side of fear and by using love, I can resolve the issue.

- I respond slowly and clearly, in a calm fashion, and from a place of love.

This is just one example of what a positivity plan can look like. The positivity plan is meant to take you out of your negative emotions and detail the steps required to respond with positivity, a reaction that is based in the love side of the emotional continuum.

Does this sound a little bit odd, crazy, or artificial? It sure could feel that way. But just like a business plan, your emotional plan needs to follow a process, a procedure that will help you be very clear about where you're starting along your negative emotional continuum and how you plan to get to a positive resolution.

Once you have your positivity plan in place, the battle to move from fear to love is halfway over. Just recognize that doing what you need to do to change your reaction is a significant accomplishment, of which you should be exceedingly proud.

The next step in the process is to practice, practice, practice, and when you think you're done practicing, practice some more. It is commonly said that it takes 28 days to change a habit or to cement a new behavior. And if you're like most people, you will be confronted in those 28 days with the behavioral triggers that will elicit the negative emotion that you are trying to transform.

To get through this behavioral change for yourself, you must be completely and utterly conscious of the change you are attempting to make. There are a number of ways to help yourself remember your positive emotional responses, and you probably already have specific ways that you remind yourself of certain things that you need to say or achieve. However, if you're looking for a few ways to help you remember to practice the positive emotions that are part of your positivity plan, here's a short list:

- Recite your plan as soon as you wake up each morning.
- Write the positive emotion on your bathroom mirror so you see it each day and associate it with yourself.
- Post the positive emotion in your office or on your cube.
- Listen to music that represents the emotion you are trying to cement.
- Create an image that you can look at to remind yourself of the positivity you are bringing into your life.
- Wear a piece of jewelry that you can touch as a gentle reminder to remain positive.
- Reward yourself with a special treat each time you respond in accordance with your positivity plan.
- Set aside a time each day to meditate on the positive emotion you are trying to bring forward in your life.

Charles Swindoll's famous quote "Attitude" has made a significant difference in the lives of so many people, so we offer it to you here in the hope that it may also inspire you to make positive changes in your life.

"The longer I live, the more I realize the impact of attitude on life.

Attitude, to me, is more important than facts. It is more important than the past, than education, than money, than circumstances, than failures, than successes, than what other people think or say or do. It is more important than appearance, giftedness or skill. It will make or break a company... a church... a home.

The remarkable thing is we have a choice every day regarding the attitude we will embrace for that day. We cannot change our past... we cannot change the fact that people will act in a certain way. We cannot change the inevitable. The only thing we can do is play on the one string we have, and that is our attitude... I am convinced that life is 10 percent what happens to me and 90 percent how I react to it.

And so it is with you... we are in charge of our attitudes."

Now, that's a quote full of positivity and a great reminder that positive reactions are fueled by the attitude we take, the reactions we have in our consciousness to live a life that is happy, healthy, and productive.

Emotions are tough to manage, but they're even harder when you are moving from negativity to positivity, allowing yourself to live more along the love side of emotional continuum than you do along the fear side. After all, you're just a human being, just like the rest of us, with all of the same emotional ups and downs, ins and outs, and unpredictability that is represented along the emotional continuum.

However, as a manager, you have a great deal of responsibility to ensure that your emotions do not get in the way of your team's ability to produce, your company's ability to succeed, or your ability to live a happy life. So, the responsibility lies with you to ensure that as you practice the change that you want to have in your emotional reaction to specific situations. You may not be able to transform from negative to positive on your own.

Ask your significant other, child, spouse, your manager, or even the members of your team to help you eradicate the negative emotions that you are attempting to remove from your life. You could be honest with all of these people by letting them know that you have identified a reaction that is not serving you, your team, or the relationships in which you participate, and that you are attempting to change. You can ask each and every one of the people in your life to point out to you that you are reacting with the identified negative emotion as it occurs, and also ask them to help you to shift your reaction to the positive emotion that you are attempting to cement.

There is absolutely no shame in asking for help. When you struggle, the only way to move to a smooth situation is for others to help you. Humans are social beings, and it is often said that we are 80 percent emotional and 20 percent analytical (IQ), which means that 80% of our interactions with others are based in emotions (EQ).

You will be pleasantly surprised that when you ask for help, people will deliver the type of help that you need. When it comes to emotions, however, especially negative emotions, you have to receive feedback without getting upset. Remember, when you ask for help, you have to be completely open to receiving it, even if it doesn't come in the form in which you would most like to see it.

Embrace Your Managerial Responsibilities

Many managers take on a management position under false assumptions. Their motivations in taking the position are fairly suspect, because they're assuming that they will have a great deal of power or make huge amounts of money. They imagine they'll revel in their authority to hire, make budget decisions, force someone to do work in a certain way, and fire at will. But those are the worst kinds of managers. They're the ones people hate, and never move very far up the managerial chain. They don't make it because they just don't get that being a manager is much more like being a catalyst for employees to experience great success, a team to achieve its goals, and a company to win in the market.

At its core, management is a helping profession. As a matter of fact, helping other people is going to make up the vast majority of what you do as a manager. You help your people get the job, improve their performance, and even transition out of the company with dignity and grace.

We've said it before and we're going to keep on saying it because it's both true and critically important for you as a new manager to understand: People leave their bosses, not their jobs. As a manager, it's your responsibility to make sure that the good people who work for your company stay with the company and continue to add value. The way that you accomplish that is to demonstrate your full commitment to your team members, every day.

Sure, you can be that manager who tells people what to do, criticizes every job they deliver, and acts mostly like a jerk that no one will follow, but isn't it better to set your sights on being the type of manager who is fully committed to other people's success and dedicated to helping them achieve?

When you help a member of your team succeed in his or her job, your whole team performs better as a group, and you're able to achieve greater success. And while that may be an obvious "win," the "win" that you might not see is this: When you help someone with something, they tend to be more loyal and committed.

Ultimately, if this is how you choose to approach your role, you will be one of those managers whom other managers look to for advice, whom employees want to work for, and whom leaders admire for your commitment and service. But even more importantly, you will be able to live a life that is much happier because you will approach your role from love instead of fear, as we discussed in previous chapters.

To achieve all of this, you first and foremost have to develop effective employee relationships. One way to do just that is by being exceptionally good at your role as a manager of others.

Hire All Tens

One of the biggest decisions you will make as manager is the decision to hire a new member of your team. This is not a decision that should be taken lightly, as it's one that will have a significant impact on your team and its ability to work well together.

Hiring can make or break all of the work that you've put into the relationships you've developed across the company. If you do it well, your manager is likely to notice and reward your abilities to seek out the right talent. If you do it wrong, you could leave him or her wondering just what you were thinking when you gave the green light.

Payroll is a huge expense for most corporations. As a result, a great deal of effort usually goes into the recruiting and hiring process, to ensure that once someone is hired, he or she is the right person for the job. Choosing the right candidate for the job, and including your team in the decision, is a big first step in building effective relationships at work.

The majority of Human Resources teams will have a standard recruiting process, interview methodology, and will provide all of the administrative support you will need to get a person up and running. But while companies will offer interview training, most don't go beyond the basics, which is very odd since hiring new employees is such a significant investment for any successful business.

As a new manager, you'll want to understand your company's overall hiring cycle, as well as how you fit into each part of the process. Knowing how the process works and following it will help your new hire have a good experience, which will set the stage for a good relationship with you once on the job.

Open a job requisition: The job requisition—aka "job req"—is a fancy way of saying that the company has an open job to which candidates may apply. In many companies, even getting the job req open can be a real challenge. Who does it? How does it get approved? Which roles get priority?

You could ask your manager, but the sad truth is that your manager may not be all that helpful either, because the likelihood is that he or she hasn't hired the volume of employees that would make the process second nature.

Your best first step is to take a trip over to the recruiting department and talk to a recruiter about the process that your company follows.

In almost all companies, your role will be to first prove to your manager that you need to either fill a position someone has left or to fill a newly created role on your team. If you are replacing a former employee, then it is likely that you will have far less to do to convince your manager that the role needs to be filled, since it is already part of the budget and approved at all levels in the organization.

However, if you are creating a new job and expanding your payroll, you need to convince your manager that the role is one that is required and a good investment for your team. Then you will want to come to your manager with the following items:

- *Job description*: Get a copy of your organization's standard job description from a recruiter and draft a job description that mirrors the template.

  Some companies do not have a standard template for defining a job description. Generally speaking, there are some standard ways that companies list job responsibilities: The first standard is to list the job tasks in priority order, with the most important task listed at the top, followed by the next most important, and so on and so forth. The second approach is to list the task that takes the most time first, followed by the next most time-intensive task, and so on.

  In these cases, a best practice for you is to create your own template—either task-based or time-based as described above—so that in the future, when you transition into a new company that has standards, you will not have a shock to the system in terms of changing the way you work. You can even go online to a job site to see how other companies set up their job descriptions and use their approach, so that you are not starting from scratch.

- *Budget*: Before you make your pitch to your manager, take a trip to the compensation department and ask a compensation specialist to price the job based on the job description you've written. If there are similar roles that already exist in your company, which require similar level of experience and education, it is likely that the specialist can give you a compensation range right away.

  However, if this is a new role in your organization, then your compensation department will likely go to an external source for compensation data and offer you a salary range at a later date. Be sure to ask the compensation specialist for the total cost, which would include salary, benefits, taxes, and any other costs that contribute to the employment of a person in this new role, because your manager will want to understand the full financial picture so that he or she can make the best decision on behalf of the company.

- *Logistics*: All corporations are in business to make a profit, and even most non-profit and governmental entities don't have the resources to have a lot of extra people running around without full workloads.

  Demonstrate to your manager that you've thought through all the details of the hire you're requesting by presenting a plan outlining the logistics of the job, as well. Show where you plan to have this person sit—either on site or in a home office. If other employees need to move to accommodate a new hire, be ready with some solid advice on how best to accomplish that task. Even if your manager doesn't say so, you can be sure he or she appreciates the thinking and effort you put into the proposal before you stop by their office to pitch it.

- *Back-up plan*: If your boss doesn't go for your plan, be sure that you have your back-up plan ready to review with him or her right there in that exact meeting.

  Your back-up plan shows what will happen if you don't get to hire your new team member. It should include what you will be forced to do less of or stop doing all together under the current set of priorities your team is tasked with achieving. If your boss still doesn't agree with the back-up plan, then you should clearly state that he or she will likely have to reset your team's priorities so that they can achieve the stated goals with the people and resources that you have in place. Invite your boss to be part of the solution so that he or she owns the outcome as much as you. When you don't have the right number of people in place to do the work, the outcome will be eroded employee relationships.

Once you have the job requisition approved and your manager has signed off on your vision for the position, either you will be assigned a recruiter who will identify candidates for the job or you will be asked to do it yourself.

If you are assigned a recruiter, feel free to lean on that person to find resumes of qualified candidates, but don't rely on that person 100 percent. Go out there to your network and ask for referrals.

There are three types of candidates:

- *Active:* Active candidates are those people who are actively seeking employment. These candidates may already be employed, but they are also serious about making a change.

- *Passive:* Passive candidates are those individuals who are not looking for a new employment opportunity. These candidates are mostly happy in their current role.

- *Employee referrals:* Probably the best type of candidate you can get is a candidate who was referred by an internal colleague whom you respect. Referred employees may be either active or passive, but they tend to be the best hires because they are known and validated by a current employee.

  The basic premise here is that good people—just like dogs—run in packs. So, if you know someone at your company who is exceptionally talented, ask him or her to refer a candidate for your open req.

Review resumes: Once you have received a big stack of resumes for the job, either you or the recruiter will be responsible for reviewing the bunch to identify the best candidates. If your recruiter is exceptionally skilled in finding candidates that are a good fit, leave the recruiter to filter the stack.

But if you are a manager who wants a little more control over the process, first check in with yourself to see why being in control is so important. Look back to previous chapters for more help with that. You can always ask to see all of the resumes and choose the top ten candidates who would then move on to the phone-screening step if you need that level of control.

The benefits of having the recruiter perform the initial screenings are in time saved for you. The potential drawback, however, is that the recruiter may only look for a one-to-one fit with the job description, meaning that he or she may only look for candidates who have the exact requirements written on the job description. Not all employees express their experience in the same way, and as an authority in the field, you would be able to account for variances.

A recruiter may miss an ideal candidate because a certain key word or specific type of job is not listed within the candidate's description of his or her experience. The best solution is to form an effective relationship with the recruiter and work as a team through the process.

Screen applicants: Once you and the recruiter have identified the top candidates, the next step of the process is to arrange a brief phone interview with each of them.

This is a good place to step back and let the recruiter take over, if you have that kind of support, because it takes a lot of time to schedule phone meetings with candidates. The role you can play to help this step be highly effective is to determine the exact questions you would like asked, as well as the answers you are hoping to hear.

At the end of this step of the hiring process, ask your recruiter to put together an overview report of each candidate with a "go" or "no-go" recommendation to move on to the next round, which will be in-person interviews.

In-Person Interview: Bringing a candidate in to talk is the beginning of the formal interview process. Although as the manager you will be making the hiring decision, this is a great time to invite the highest performing employees on your team to participate in the interviewing process.

A good manager will invite his or her best team members into the process and allow them to influence the hiring decision, because the team's point of view counts. If you do end up making a hire against their better advice, be sure to follow up with them to provide all of the reasons for your decision.

Why limit participation to your best performing team members? Because these employees are going to have an uncanny ability to sense how well a candidate is likely to perform. Also, you don't want these top performers to pull back because they are not happy with the new hire.

You may also want to consider adding your boss to the interview team, as well as others who might need to have a close working relationship with the person on the role. This demonstrates your commitment to fostering effective employee relationships. But be sure you keep your interview team small! When the team gets too big, you'll end up with far too many opinions to matter and run the risk of disappointing a lot of people. You may also overwhelm the candidate with a large interview team and cause an otherwise great potential employee to be disinterested.

Once you have your interview team in place, work with your recruiter to determine the number of rounds of interviews that will take place for this role. It is recommended that you never have more than three rounds:

- *Round one, skill assessment*: As the manager, you should be the very first person to interview the candidate to assess his or her skill set. Use the first round of in-person interviews to determine what skills each candidate brings to the table. You might want to invite one or two team members (again, only the highest performing members of your team) to participate with you, but be sure that each member of the team is asking different questions so that you get the most—and best—information out of the interview.

To facilitate success, meet with members of the team prior to the first-round interviews to ensure that each of you are clear as to the questions you will ask, as well as the purpose behind each question.

In addition, first round interviews are a good time for you as a manager to take time to understand how the candidate likes to be managed and what he or she has disliked about previous managers. Be sure, too, that you are clearly communicating your management style in order to evaluate whether there's a good fit between the two of you.

Finally, remember that you and your team are being interviewed and evaluated by the candidate, as well. We've all been through interviews where we are asked the same question over and over again, which is not fun for the candidate and a colossal waste of time for the first-round interviewers. Only five to six of the top ten candidates who pass the phone screen should move into the interview process.

- *Round two, personality and culture fit*: By this interview round, you should have narrowed the field down to three or four of the candidates from the original five or six. For this part of the process, the potential candidate should meet with the interviewers with whom he or she will work most closely. You should not need to interview the candidate again during this round, unless you have additional questions that popped up after the first round. Instead, ask others to get in there and get to know their potential co-worker. Just be sure to at least great the candidate and walk him or her out once the interviews are over so that you have the opportunity to demonstrate your interest in the candidate's success in the process and show that you are the type of good manager who is always available for their people.

During this round, make sure that each of your team members are asking different questions and that everyone understands the purpose behind the questions they are asking. Encourage your interviewers to delve deep into each candidate's likes and dislikes related to the working environment, commute, hours, work style, benefits, etc.

- *Round three, sell the job*: By the time you get to the third round of interviews, you should have selected your top two candidates, representing the best of the best.

  The final round of interviews should be conducted by you, your boss, and perhaps the senior executive who is responsible for your business unit. This last conversation isn't about skills or personality fit, because you should already feel confident that the candidates who have made it this far would function very well on your team. Instead, this final interview should be entirely about selling the candidate into the job. It should be an inspirational interview that leaves the candidate wanting to join the company and ready to say "yes" to an employment offer.

Offer the job: Before you make your offer to your chosen candidate, gather feedback from each member of the interview team as soon as they have completed the interview. Or ask your company's recruiter to solicit that feedback for you.

Your natural inclination might be just to make the decision on your own, based on your own perspective, experience, and insights, but this isn't the best practice for those who aspire to develop effective employee relationships.

Remember that your team members have been part of this process—at your invitation. To discount their input now makes the effort they've made in helping you find an ideal candidate seem wasted. In addition, remember that your existing team is likely to be the set of people working most closely with your new hire, and you want to ensure peak performance for your team from the moment the new hire arrives.

You'll also want to ask your boss for his or her final input. Armed with all this information, it's time to make your final decision. Once you have everyone's input, make the best decision you can on behalf of the interview team.

Then, meet with the recruiter to develop a job offer and get that offer to the prospective employee. Even though larger corporations will ask the recruiter to manage the entire job offer procedures, once the offer is made, be sure to reach out to the candidate to answer any final questions and sell the candidate into the job quickly.

And when your prospective new team member has accepted the job offer, be sure to follow up with each member of the interview team to announce your hiring decision and the date your new employee will start. This is also a good time to go back and have a follow-up conversation with anyone who didn't agree with the hiring decision, to see if you can bring them around to your way of thinking. If you can't persuade them, at least leave them with a clear understanding about the hiring decision you made.

Rejection notices: One of the most overlooked and often forgotten steps in the hiring process is following up with those candidates who were rejected at various stages of the interview process. Unfortunately, because of what we feel are often nonsensical employment laws, most companies will not allow any member of the interview team to offer the candidate feedback. Even if your company's policy is not to offer feedback, you still can reach out to those candidates who were interviewed to personally thank them for their participation and give encouragement about reapplying for future positions. You will want to do this for two reasons: You might just need to call one of them back in the near future to ask him or her to join your team, and you also never know who you might be working with, or asking for a job from, in your own professional future. So, it is in your best interest to treat every person that you interview with a great deal of dignity and respect. This is the human thing to do too.

Which brings us to our final note on the hiring process: Most of us will rate an employee on a scale from one to ten, where ten is the best of the best. A ten will hire another ten, but a nine will hire an eight, an eight will hire a seven, and so on.

Don't let this be true for you. As a manager, you want the best people with the best skills around you all of the time, because that's how you ensure that you and your team are performing at optimal levels. So, if you are a nine, seek to hire a ten. Find someone who puts your skills to shame and let that candidate soar with success on your team. Why? Because in the world of business today, exceptional talent is exceptionally hard to find and if you can find it, then you have no other option but to succeed. Don't let fear of someone outshining you be your motivation for hiring inadequate employees.

Warmly Welcome New Hires

Everyone has been a new employee at some time or another. It's a tough spot to be in. You are faced with learning the ins and outs of a large number of new processes, policies, and procedures, and that's on top of spending a lot of time and energy developing new relationships, all the while hoping you can remember where the bathroom is.

If you are a manager who only hires the best of the best, that means you need to make a personal commitment to getting your new hire off to the best start possible because highly productive employees expect nothing less.

The best thing you can do for a new hire is to have an onboarding plan that begins on the first day of his or her employment and extends through the next ninety days on the job.

We call this the "ramp-up" period, and if done right, it will take as much time, focus, and energy from you as it does your new hire. You'll be offering both coaching and encouragement to your new hires, who need to feel your confidence in their abilities and leave every day feeling exceptionally good about what they've accomplished in their new positions.

If you're working for a larger company, there's probably a formal orientation program already in place that tends to take one or two days to complete. More often than not, these programs focus on providing candidates with a company overview and filling out required paperwork. If you're in a business where security is a concern, ensuring that new hires get badges on their first day is a priority. In other words, there won't be a lot of information that's useful for your new hire to get into the swing of things with your team.

That leaves you, as a manager, with a lot of work to do to get your new hire up and running. Here are a few winning activities that should do the trick:

1. *Write a ramp-up plan*: Develop a plan for your new hire to follow for the first 90 days on the job, It should include what he or she needs to learn, such as specific company jargon, information technology systems, people, and team priorities.

2. *Make introductions*: Spend time walking your new team member around the company to introduce him or her to everyone and anyone who the new hire may come in contact with in the first 90 days on the job. Also bring your new hire to meetings with you so that he or she can get a feeling for how people work together and to get first-hand experience with the power players.

3. *Assign a buddy*: Some companies have a new hire buddy program in place, but if your company doesn't use a formal program, ask someone on your team to pal around with the new hire. One of the most important retention elements beyond the relationship that an employee has with his manager is the relationships he or she has with co-workers.

4. *Meet one-on-one*: For the first 90 days that your new hire is on the job, meet one-on-one each week to talk about what's working and what's not and to

review progress. The relationship that you have with your new hire is critically important to both of your success, so take this time to develop your relationship seriously. Consider these meetings to be sacred and stick to them with a firm commitment. Don't move, cancel, or ask to reschedule the meeting.

Above all, celebrate your new hire. Find "wins" for your new hire to achieve right from the start. For example, if your new hire is responsible for sales, help him or her close a deal in the first month. Or, if your new hire is responsible for accounts payable, help him or her to cut checks without mistakes. Whatever the job may be, find a way to help the new hire build confidence by doing great work and then give all of the credit to the new hire for the achievement.

You can also give your new hire a very warm welcome by sending out a broad introductory e-mail to your entire organization. This e-mail should be full of personality and fun, and focus on the knowledge, skills, and abilities the new hire brings to the team, as well as his or her professional background. Add in lots of human elements to the note, as well. For example, if your new hire is married with three kids, a dog, a cat, and a parakeet, communicate that. People enjoy knowing others beyond the work they do together. Humans are social beings, so that note should be written in a meaningful and social way, too.

One note of caution, however: Be sure the new hire has an opportunity to read the note before it is sent. Using the above example, the new hire might be in the middle of an ugly divorce, so the acknowledgment of a spouse might be awkward or inappropriate.

One way to ensure that you're getting to know your employee is by having him or her answer a few human interest questions. Do this by developing a new employee in-take form to know your employee's personal likes and dislikes. The items below are just a few examples of questions your form can include:

1. Tell me ten things about yourself we may not know.

2. What do you like to do for fun outside of work?

3. How do you like to be rewarded for a job well done?

4. Do you get embarrassed by public recognition?

All things considered, your goal in welcoming a new hire to the team is to reinforce the fact that he or she made the right decision to join your team and the company.

Having an excellent onboarding plan fuels your opportunity to have an effective relationship with your new hire. A solid plan will also set up the new hire to develop effective relationships with others.

Set Goals

It's a common practice at most companies to ask employees to state their "goals" for the year. It's equally common for those goals to end up being completely ignored for the remainder of the year—at least until the time for a performance review rolls around.
There's often a real gap between what HR is asking employees to do and the actual set of goals that employees state. But, that's where you come in, master manager.

Even though, in asking employees to state their professional goals, HR is erring on the side of good, most of the time employees don't see it that way at all. Instead, most see the exercise as a waste of time and worry that if they fail to meet the goals they've stated—no matter what the circumstances—that will only end up being used against them at performance review time. Why? Because that's pretty much what happens.

Company priorities change, especially if you are in a company that experiences high growth, poor revenue, or continual crisis, which is most companies. As a result, employees are commonly asked by those in charge to work on new and different priorities than the ones they stated as their goals, and then later find themselves criticized for not achieving what they set out to do.

Your job is to start the goal-setting process by helping your employees write goals that make sense for them. As a manager, you can break that unpleasant cycle for your employees, and get a good start at it by doing exactly what HR is asking for you to do—get the goals set.

What HR fails to communicate is that your goals, and your employees' goals, can be updated every day if you or they want to spend time doing it.

There are a number of formulas that you can use to write goals, but the best goals tend to be aligned to your team's stated priorities; are measureable, achievable, and realistic; and are bound by time. For example, if you're in any kind of customer service industry, you might encourage one of your team members to set a goal of answering 30 customer calls per day each month. These kinds of measurable, achievable, and realistic goals are often termed SMART goals. Paul J Meyer describes the characteristics of SMART goals in *Attitude is Everything*. (Meyer)

Productivity goals are expected, but if you're concerned that your employees may not have the skills required to achieve your team's priorities by the end of the year, you can use the goal-setting process as a time to figure out how they will acquire those skills.

If the goals don't hit the mark, then you've got to go back to your employees and make sure you're covering your bases so you can achieve your priorities as a team.

If you need a particular employee to add specific activities to his or her goals for the year, a one-on-one meeting will work best. If you have a set of employees who basically perform the same tasks and there are tasks not getting done, go back to the entire team to ask for volunteers to take on the missing tasks from the team's list of collective goals.

Of course, it is important to note that if you add something in then you should definitely take something away. Your employees have a small number of hours to work each day. So, if all you do is add priorities to your team's list of responsibilities, then they will have so much to do that little will get done in a given period of time. So, when you add to your employee's list of to-do's, you have to either 1.) Hire your employee an assistant who can help get the work done or 2.) Remove items on the list to make room for the new assignments.

Don't be afraid to dig deep into the goals your employees send you for review. This is your opportunity to do an in-depth review of your team's actual abilities and areas of productivity and get every single one of the members of your team pointed in the right direction and working on only those things that are important.

This is also your time to review the actual knowledge, skills, and abilities that your team has, both as individuals and as a group. You may find that some employees need to learn new ways of doing business, acquire new skills, or even up-level their unique abilities. This is also an excellent time to have your employees declare their own career development goals. Combining the two activities is a win-win opportunity, as it better enables you to guide your team toward your final destination and help your employees grow their careers.

Measure Performance to Increase Productivity

Employees and managers alike tend to seriously dislike performance reviews for a lot of the same reasons. However, you can use performance reviews to improve the effectiveness of your relationships with employees.

Performance reviews take a lot of time, the feedback comes too late to be actionable, and no one really agrees on performance ratings. Instead of performance reviews being of help to employees, often times reviews tend to be used against them, keep something from them, or take something away from them. Given how deeply unpopular the whole process is, it's almost comical then that so many companies continue to use archaic performance systems, particularly given that they don't help the company to achieve its strategy.

If the company you work for requires standard performance reviews, expect to be heavily involved in the process. Performance reviews tend to occur along a set period of time. Your HR team will let you know the deadlines you'll need to meet and may even offer training to help you write and deliver performance reviews.

The secret to an effective performance review isn't in what you write down, the final rating you give, or even the training you might get to deliver it. Instead, what makes a performance review both fair and effective is the accurate reflection of feedback you've provided to your employee day in and day out through the performance period.
Daily performance feedback doesn't need to be written in a formal document or a special conversation; you can give informal feedback on what your employees deliver and how they deliver it every day if you like. A lot of the time, it's enough to let an employee simply know that he or she has done "a great job," or that he or she "needs to step it up a notch."

Even if your feedback is informal as described above, be sure that you're documenting that feedback, so you are able to track performance improvements and monitor issues over periods of time. So, for example, if an employee does a great job on a project, offer that feedback verbally during a one-on-one meeting, and then document what you told the employee and save it either in a physical or an electronic file.

When performance review season comes around, you can just cut and paste the content you already have, with specific examples that the employee has already received, into the official performance review form. Documenting feedback will not only help you reflect accurate performance during a review, it will also save you a lot of time in preparation.

The important takeaway here, though, is this: Employees should never be surprised by the feedback you provide about their performance. Giving feedback all year long helps you manage performance and continuously drive up productivity. If you have an employee who performs exceptionally well, then the formal performance review will serve as a confirmation of that performance. Conversely, if you have an employee who underperforms, then you will have a host of specific examples of poor performance that you can use to illustrate the employee's specific areas of weakness.

And if that terrible day arrives when you have to fire an employee, you will have all of the documentation that HR will require of you to do the deed. While firing someone may be one of the hardest actions you'll ever have to take as a manager, it is often a win-win situation. It is a win for the employee because he or she is released to find a role that better fits his or her individual career interests. It is a win for the company because you can fill the role with an individual who is able to deliver the type of performance you require.

The worst part of every performance review isn't the fact that you will spend a heck of a lot of time writing them and assigning a performance rating. The worst part is that you will then send the review and rating up the chain for approval. Why? Because a controversial (and we think, ultimately detrimental) part of the traditional performance review is the fact that a lot of companies use a performance curve that allows for only a very small number of employees to be rated as "top performers."

The problem here is that, even if you rate someone in the very top bucket of performance, your manager or someone along the way may decide to change it simply because the performance you're documenting has to fit a distribution curve.

The terrible news is that the now-deflated performance rating is then used to calculate a bonus or salary increase. As a result, the employee who you see as delivering exceptional performance is then assigned a bonus that is inconsistent with the exceptional contributions you recognized in your performance review. What makes this incredibly tough is that you're the one who gets to deliver the bad news, not the person who made the change somewhere up the management chain.

But never fear! If you feel that this injustice has happened to someone on your team, you can always talk to your manager and your HR representative to attempt to do what is right for your employee. If you can't get them to change the rating, ask your manager to deliver the performance review with you and to explain to the employee why the rating was deflated. Now, this is a risky strategy, because as a manager your company will lean on you to deliver bad news all the time and you'll be required to do it.

To help repair the damaged trust this situation may cause, look for other ways to give the employee something of value. Offer career development, an expanded role, or more responsibility and tie all of that to the possibility of greater compensation in the future...and then stick to your word, or you will do more even damage to the relationship in the future.

Complete Your Approvals—Fast

One of the biggest moments that you will have as a manager is when you realize that you don't have the final say on most business decisions. But, your company will ask you time and again to approve everything from expense reports and time off, to performance ratings and bonus recommendations. More importantly, your employees will look to you to quickly approve their requests and submissions; and if you don't meet their expectations, the effective manager-employee relationship that you've worked so hard to build will degrade.

Right from your very first role as a manager of people, you need to get very comfortable with the fact that your manager, your manager's manager, and management all the way up to the chief executive officer of your organization are all people who have the power to override your decisions. Everyone has a manager, and not every manager is a good one or takes the time to check in with you to understand the reasons behind the approvals that you are making, to ensure that they are consistent with standard business practices.

There are a plethora of items that you will be asked to approve. The most common are:

- Job descriptions
- Job requisitions
- Job postings
- Job offers
- Budgets
- Performance reviews
- Performance ratings
- Career development plans
- Expense reports
- Paid time off
- Employee gifts
- Bonuses
- Stock offers
- Salary increases

You will be asked to approve items like those listed here for each of your employees. As a result, you can bet that you'll be spending a great deal of time reviewing requests, sending questions back to employees for clarification, and sending your approval up the management chain for final confirmation of the very approval you have already made.

To be a productive manager of approvals, you will need to be exceptionally organized. With technology increasing the speed of your employee's requests for approvals, your employees will expect that as soon as they hit "send" you will hit "approve."

No matter how unreasonable it may be to believe that any one person who manages multiple employees would be able to instantly approve any type of approval request, your employees may perceive your role as one that functions to support and approve their work at any given time of day, night, or even over the weekend.

One of the best ways you can ensure these requests are being approved in a timely fashion is to set aside an hour a week to review any requests for approvals that have come across your desk. Now, that doesn't mean that the hour happens all at once.

This is truly one of those times when having solid time management skills will help you as a manager, not just in making your employees happy, but also in keeping the business humming along.

Bottom line—don't allow your own time management issues to delay timely approvals. If you do, your team will let you know that you are unable to meet their expectations by most likely imprinting a great, big, red "FAIL" stamp on your forehead. The telltale signs that you are not working in a timely enough fashion include: An increase in your team's frustration level, a decrease in communication, and a general lack of enthusiasm for new projects.

Offer Training to Boost Skills

Everyone needs training. You need it, your team needs it, your boss needs it, and it's not a risky bet to assume that your CEO also needs training. Having solid skills helps to increase the respect and credibility we apply to one another; and credibility and respect contribute to the development of effective employee relationships.

Before we jump into the ins and outs of training, it is important to take just a moment and point out the fact that your HR team will likely call training something other than "training." Words to watch out for include development, learning, and the ever so popular, University. No matter what HR calls it, however, at the end of the day if humans are learning new skills, they are indeed receiving training.

In your role as a manager, you will be doing yourself, your team, and the company a good service if you dedicate a certain portion of your year to training. This is one point where most managers completely miss the mark.

Employees often believe that they are too busy to get additional training, mostly because their manager does not prioritize it for them. Managers, reacting to the intense pressure from above to produce, produce, produce, and often do not stop to consider the fact that if they spent some time training their employees, the level of production would go up, and thus the pressure from the top would go down. What does all this mean? Make time for yourself and for your team to get additional training. When you do set aside even a small percentage of hours for yourself and your team, you are guaranteed better results.

Training for you, as for anyone else in your company, can come in three ways: in the classroom, on-the-job, and through relationships, such as mentoring. It is likely that you will gain the most benefit from training that occurs on-the-job or through relationships with people who can guide you in the right direction, based on their own personal experiences.

You already know your skills, and most managers only need to go to a class once to learn how to do a specific task. So, it's probably going to be more beneficial for you to work on attaining the kind of "softer skills" you can learn through working with a mentor. Identify someone in your organization who you admire and ask him or her if they'd be interested in being your mentor. See the section on mentoring earlier in this book.

In addition, always look for opportunities to learn on the job and recognize that, as you learn new things in your role as a manager, indeed you are getting trained. After all, you didn't know it before you had the experience and now you do, and it is likely that the best experiences you have during your day far outshine any type of classroom work that you could complete.

Everything we've outlined above holds just as true for your employees as it does for you.

Your employees will get a heck of a lot of on-the-job training just by doing their jobs, making and correcting mistakes, and asking lots of questions.

They might find a mentor, but it's more likely that they will want to attend conferences to learn from others in their trade. And it's never a bad idea to send your employees to specialized classes that will allow them to gain specific skills your team can use to meet its stated goals.

Some companies will ask you to create a career development plan for each member of your team.

Other companies will ask the employees to do this career development plan for themselves. There is no right or wrong way to approach development and training, but it is important that everyone—from the CEO down to the interns—own their own development, particularly because corporations are not always as loyal to employees as employees are to be corporations.

Be sure you own your own career and you get the training you need, so your employees receive the benefit of your wisdom. Even if your organization does not require a plan, be sure to make a simple list of skills that each person in your team would like to learn that year and document a plan to help them meet their training goals. Investing in the development of your employees demonstrates your commitment to their success, which fuels the effectiveness of your employee relationships.

Take Breaks to Avoid Burnout

Who doesn't like a vacation? Think about it. Where do you want to go right now? Hawaii? Japan? Maybe spend a little time on the French Riviera? While all of those are exceptionally great ideas, many people don't take time to get away from the office to take a vacation—your employees included!

Of course, one of your chief responsibilities as a manager is to ensure that the work that your team is responsible for delivering is in fact delivered with quality. However, because they're only human, if the members of your team don't have a moment to relax, unwind, and chill out, you are guaranteed to not deliver on your team's goals in a way that is happy, healthy, and indeed productive.

That's why, in your role as a manager, it is critically important that you monitor the accrued vacation time that each of your employees has in the bank and make sure your people are taking the time off that they need. Helping employees get away from it all proves your interest in their mental health, a statement that will support the development of effective relationships.

One way to accomplish this is to create a rough "vacation time threshold" and once the members of your team cross that threshold, you sit down and talk to them about taking a vacation.

Get to know how each member of your team handles stress so that you can forecast when they may need a vacation most. This is an art, it's not a science. Sometimes you're going to get this exactly right and others you're going to fail miserably. The point is to be consciously aware that you need to monitor vacation time used.

Just the simple act of sitting down and talking with your team about taking a needed break will likely result in a great deal of respect from them. Again, management is a helping profession, which includes helping someone see the brick wall they are about to run into even when they don't see it themselves.

When people are operating in a fast-paced or high stress environment, they tend to burn out very quickly. That's true for you, and it's true for your team.

The easiest way to ensure that each member of your team is indeed getting out to take a vacation is to simply create a vacation calendar and ask everyone to submit the days they want off. Then, reinforce your support of your employees taking a vacation. Once you have the calendar set up, pull it out at the beginning of every quarter during a team meeting and review the time that each person will be taking off and talk about how other employees can help to cover their workload during that period.

There is one great, big, important fact that you need to know about vacation time: In certain companies, vacation time is considered a cash asset. The employee earns it. While this publication is not intended to be a legal guide for managers, you can always check in with your HR representative to find out what the laws are in the location in which you work. If your company is bound by such a policy, HR may require your employees to take time off so that the company reduces its cash liability.

Focus on Finishing

You have a lot of work to do in your role as a manager. Not only will you have your own workload, which is never ending, but now you have responsibility for other people, which means a significantly increased responsibility to the company.

And the best news of all is that when you have exceptionally good time management skills, you can get it all done. You can always delegate some of your functional workload to senior members of your team when you have managerial tasks that increase during certain periods of time. Or, ensure that you are doing little bits of your managerial responsibilities all throughout the year so when you need to make a big push, you're prepared far in advance of your deadline. It's up to you, but you can do it.

Management is one of the most fulfilling roles that anyone will ever play in business. You get to help others, you get to help the team, and in doing all of that, you often get to help yourself, too. So, when you get all of the work done that the company is asking you to do and you do so in a timely manner, you will gain the respect and admiration not just of your employees, but of your fellow managers and everyone up your managerial chain as well. It is this respect that serves as one of the many building blocks in the foundation of employee relationships.

So… get it done!

Find Meaning through Strategic Alignment

One of the best ways you can build an effective relationship with your employees is to help them find meaning at work. Everyone is looking for it in their own special way. Since we spend at least a third of our waking adult life at work, finding meaning through the work that one does day in and day out can be exceptionally rewarding.

One of the best ways to help your employees find meaning in life through work is to ensure that they are only working on what's important. The great news here is that you can help your employee to find this meaning, help yourself to lead your team in the delivery of exceptional results, and help your company succeed, by simply aligning the work that is done under your watch with your company's strategy.

As a manager of people, you can do a lot of good for everyone if you get very clear about where your company is going, how it is going to get there, and your team's role in all of that. In fact, it's your job—no, it's your ethical responsibility—to make decisions that fuel your company's success, your team's success, and the success of each and every individual you manage.

Functionally, what that means is that you will have to make decisions about your people and your team's priorities, organizational structure, compensation, recognition, and more. All of these decisions are based entirely on what your company has set out to achieve and the role your team will play in achieving these goals; and to help your employees find meaning through the work they do you need to get very good at understanding their individual career objectives, skills, and abilities, while spending a great deal of time coordinating teamwork so that everyone feels great about what they are doing.

The frustration for most managers comes in when they are asked to ensure that each employee has declared their goals for the year. Generally speaking, it is a waste of time to just state the goals and go about your business. Most organizations don't require goals to be aligned, and if the goals are not aligned, then what good are they anyway? Remember, since being a manager is a helping profession and you are helping employees to find meaning, then their goals must support that for meaning to become a reality.

Trust us…it is never a waste of time to ensure that the goals of your team line up behind your company's strategy, and that everyone is working only on the right set of priorities.

That said, in your role as a manager, it's your responsibility to drive high performance across your team. Let's be frank here: If you under deliver, it will certainly be held against you; and though we hate to be the ones to break it to you, you'll rarely, if ever, earn praise for exceeding what you signed up to deliver. So then, that is the other reason to ensure that your employees are working on what's most important, because you will be the one left holding the bag when it doesn't go right. And if you are left holding the bag, resentment may reduce your ability to facilitate effective employee relationships.

So…did we give you enough reasons to get into goal alignment? We promise that if you do it well, you will not only be praised as an amazing manager, but also your employees will have a clear set of deliverables that they believe in and are excited to produce for you, their rock star manager.

Focus Only on What's Important

Regardless of whether your company has a formal way to cascade its strategy or align everyone's goals, you can still drive exceptional performance across your team by ensuring that each and every employee is working on the right set of priorities. Not only will you be able to get a great deal of traction on projects, but you will also have a team that is happily producing results.

But what the heck is a strategy cascade? Well, in its simplest of terms, a strategy cascade refers to the process through which the CEO's office communicates the company's strategy to each layer of management, ending with employees. It typically starts with the CEO presenting the strategy to the people who report to him or her. These executives then create their business unit strategies, based on the CEO's company strategy, and present it to the people who report to them. Then, those individuals write their group strategy based on the business unit's strategy, which was carved out of the company strategy, which is then presented to their management teams. You can see how this could get complicated if we continued to detail this out. But you get the idea.

So how is that different from goal alignment? Well, they are pretty much two sides of the same coin. But, goal alignment is where the real action is when it comes to managing your employees and helping them to find meaning at work.

Upon the conclusion of the strategy cascade, many employers will ask employees to write goals that are firmly focused on the achievement of the strategy that was presented to them at their level. So then, executives typically have far-reaching goals; managers have goals that are written for a team of people; and individuals have goals that are very specific. And, when you add up all of the individual goals in a given company, they should collectively detail the necessary tasks needed to complete the strategy.

The purpose of goal alignment is to ensure that each employee is working only on the right set of tasks. Practically speaking, if the strategy cascade works the way it is intended, then employees should have a very good understanding of you team's responsibilities in the achievement of the company's strategy. Will they get the company's strategy based on all of these presentations? Maybe. Will they have a clear understanding of what they need to do in a given period based on their aligned goals? Definitely! And because they will only be working on important tasks, then they will most likely find more meaning, which means you did your job. Congrats!

Your company will likely put forward a lot of complex language firmly rooted in human resources jargon. They may ask you to write SMART (strategic, measureable, attainable, realistic, and time bound) goals for your team, or they may have another goal formula that is unique to the company. However the request is structured or articulated, what it lacks is solid information on *how* strategies are to be translated into goals specifically for the individuals.

There are four parts to goals development that you need to understand to ensure that you're applying the company's strategic alignment to your area of responsibility:

1. *Company strategy*: The most successful companies in the world develop their business strategy entirely based on the needs of customers. The fastest growing and most admired companies typically have a laser-like focus on customer success, which

means that their strategies have very little to do with the tactics of running a business. So, as a manager, it is your job to understand how to support the full and total implementation of this strategy while still getting your and your team's work done in the most efficient way possible. Know it inside and out, and spend time understanding your business unit's part in all of it.

2. *Business unit priorities*: Generally speaking, once the company has decided on a particular strategy, the senior-most executives begin talking about what their organizations are committed to achieving. Now, these statements are still pretty high level, but the business unit leader will typically spend time with his or her directors and managers to identify the business unit's priorities in support of the company strategy.

   For example, if one of the company's strategies is to open new markets, an IT business unit leader may make it a priority to open a data center that can serve new markets.

3. *Team goals*: The next step is for each team to carve out specific goals, based on the business unit priorities. This is where you, as the team leader, think through your team's role in achieving the business unit's priorities and then document what the team will do to achieve those priorities. Following along on the above IT example, the database team manager may create stated goals about cost savings in the identification and procurement of new equipment.

4. *Individual contributions*: The last step is to have each individual on your team state exactly what he or she will achieve in relation to the team's goals. For example, an individual would write a statement

that expresses his or her responsibilities with equipment, such as all equipment is set up and in place by February 3.

While we are only showing a cascade of four levels here, some companies—particularly those with massively overly engineered management layers—may have many more levels. Don't let layers of complexity in this kind of organization intimidate you. Instead, stay entirely focused on what your team is responsible for achieving in any given year and you will achieve amazing success.

The executive team at your company isn't going to expect you to know every detail of its strategic plan. As a matter of fact, it is highly likely that the most critical and proprietary elements of the business strategy will be held so closely to your CEO's chest that there will be no way to unclench his or her grip for you read it. It's the CEO's obligation to the company's stockholders. Don't take it personally.

That doesn't mean you can't fully understand the strategy as it is presented. Even if your company leadership is only presenting 80 percent of the overall strategy to you, what they're asking is that you focus all of your time, efforts, and energy on that 80 percent, rather than worry about the remaining 20 percent, where you probably can't have an impact. Remember, it's not uncommon for a company to share most of what it is planning instead of all of what it is planning.

If your company is one that doesn't require a strategy cascade, you will look like a hero in terms of building a team that is effective, efficient, and ready to win on behalf of your company. Did someone say promotion?

The number one most important thing you can do as a manager in relation to helping your employees find meaning is to get invited into the room when the strategy for your organization is being discussed so that you can give input up front, rather than having a strategy handed to you with the expectation that your team executes it flawlessly.

And who doesn't want to be able to give input into the work that they will be asked to do in any given year? No one. Get yourself involved right from the start so there is never a question as to your ability to support the strategic formation of the company or your team's ability to deliver.

As a manager, you are in a precarious situation when it comes to strategic alignment, mostly because you are the liaison between the executives and the employees. That means your negotiation skills must be top-notch when it comes to having everyone agree to the type of work that your employees will take on in any given year, as well as offering input up the management chain as to what is possible given the resources you have in place.

When you look up your management chain, it is likely that you will find a big, long list of people who have exceptional skills and more years of experience than your entire team combined. But don't let that intimidate you; it doesn't mean they're any good at translating the company strategy from theory to practice. That's your job as a manager of people.

Another part of your responsibility will be to give good, clear feedback on the strategy to your manager before you can get your team aligned behind it, unless of course you fully agree with the direction as it is presented to you. If that's the case, get to work and align your team. However, it is a rare day that a manager does not have a question, comment, consideration, or request for additional resources after seeing all that will be asked of his or her people.

When you truly grasp the company's strategy, the managerial tactics that will be needed to achieve it will be evident to you. If you do not clearly understand the strategy, there is no way that you will be able to identify the tactics that will be needed to achieve it.

Turn Strategy into Success

At this point, it's critical that you understand your company's strategy so you can define your tactics and apply your team's skills to meet the goals of the company. Well, that is if you want to help them discover that they have a real impact on the organization. As a manager, you have to study.

This is where you learn whether you are just an exceptionally skilled employee or truly a great manager of the business and its people. Your skills in translating from a strategic to an operational plan are tantamount to being successful, because you will be defining the tactics that your team members will employ to help the company achieve its end result. By illuminating this area of your managerial skills, we are confident you will have continued success.

Translating a strategy so that each member of your team fully understands his or her part in achieving it is no easy task. Strategies tend to be exceptionally high level and sweeping, rather than specific and actionable, and something the average Joe or Jane can understand. In our experience, most people are rarely taught how to think strategically, even if they graduate from one of the top business schools.

So when we say it takes a lot of time and energy to translate a strategy in a way that anyone can understand, we mean it. But that doesn't mean you can't master the art, and when you do, you will have mastered one of the most important skills for managers, something we like to call "making sense of it all."

Nine times out of 10, the surface of the business strategy will have little or nothing to do with your team or the responsibilities that make up individual jobs, particularly at the lowest levels of the organization.

But no matter what the level of responsibility of the team you're managing, you can have an impact on the success of your company's strategy, by employing a technique we call "Customer Back."

Earlier in this chapter, we talked about the fact that, at its essence, your company strategy has to involve making sure that the customer is satisfied, in order to be successful. So if your organization is fully focused on its customers, you should be too.

To make this technique work for you and your team, map the customer outcome to the strategy, the strategy to your organization's priorities, the priorities to your team's goals, and then show each individual employee how his or her contributions map to your team's goals. Sounds like a big job, right? Well, it is a heck of a lot easier than you would think, especially when you have a firm grasp on your company's strategy and the outcomes it hopes to achieve in a given year.

To prove our point, here's an example of how the "Customer Back" Mapping tactic works.

Step 1: On the chart below, you will find the customer column on the far left. In that space, write the question you are trying to answer in relationship to your customer. In this case, we simply ask, "What do you want to do for your customer?"

Step 2: Under the company column, answer the question you pose in the customer column. When dealing with the highest level of the strategies, such as the strategy for an entire company, this statement should be short, direct, and make a clear point. In this case, what we want to do is delight our customer.

Step 3: From there, each business unit leader spells out his or her group's responsibility in the strategy. In this case, let's say that the business unit is responsible for marketing. As such, the Marketing leadership team would determine what their group's role is in delighting our customer. For the sake of this example, let's say that their answer is to produce rock-star-like trade shows.

Step 4: Once the business unit direction is set, it is then each team's responsibility to state their role in achieving the business unit strategy. So using our example of the Marketing team and focusing on events, let's say that the Event team reports to Marketing and their part in the strategy is to provide free rock concerts at tradeshow events.

Step 5: Finally, once the team has declared its role in achieving this customer strategy, each individual can sign up for the tasks he or she is to complete to contribute to the overall strategy. In this case, the individual will hire a rock star to perform.

Customer Back Mapping Example				
Customer Outcome	Company Strategy	Business Unit Priorities	Team Goals	Individual Tasks
What do you want to do for your customer?	Delight our customer	Produce rock-star like tradeshows	Provide free rock concerts at trade-show events	Hire a rock star to perform at the concert

The above is just an example, but you should be able to see how you can translate the strategy for each and every employee in your group and for the role that they perform for your company. When you do this well, every one of your team members will understand specifically how his or her contributions impact the company's success, which is critically important for both your team member's success and your company's success. Everyone wants his or her work to mean something in this world. In fact, helping employees find that meaning at work is one of the best things that you can do as a manager. It can be rewarding for you, and it certainly will be rewarding your employees.

In some cases, you may find there is absolutely no strategic translation in the world that will work for a specific role or person on your team. This means that this individual or role is not required for your company to achieve its stated strategy, organizational priorities, or team goals. In the big picture, that means that you, as a manager, should either have that person start to work in a different role that is critical to the company's success or eliminate the role entirely. This is the dark side of strategic alignment. It's not fun, but it is necessary for you as a manager to ensure that your team is 100% aligned and focused on meeting the company's goals.

Once you've worked through the ins and outs of translating what is an exceptionally high level strategy into very specific operational tactics that your team can employ, it's time to go ahead and present it to your team. The goal of this presentation is to first and foremost ensure that all individual buy into not only the direction your company is going, but also their role in your team's goals.

That means you will have to be persuasive, especially if your team is one that will be transitioning to a whole new set of deliverables or operating procedures as a result of the new company strategy. The truth is people are often resistant to change, even if they don't know why. People naturally want their world to stay consistent. If your presentation is fraught with change, your translation skills will be even more important so that you can get them on board with what your team is going to achieve.

The presentation of the company strategy should start from the broadest, high-level perspective and narrow down to the individual contributions that you expect to be made in the coming year. Think of this approach as an inverted pyramid. The presentation would start with the highest level of the company strategy, followed by the priorities that were identified by your organization's leadership as most important in achieving that strategy, then an explicit translation of those priorities into your team's goals, and conclude with the expectations you have for every individual on your team.

Very few companies will offer its people managers a strategic goal alignment toolkit to help you achieve aligning each and every employee behind your company strategy. Most of the time, all you get is an e-mail request that you go through the process, but there will be no mention of any kind of training that might help you succeed at this. So if you're in a company that offers you a presentation toolkit, a set of information, presentation tools, training, and other related resources, consider yourself one of the lucky ones. The majority of the work to present to your team has been done for you in advance. Your job will be just to fill in the blanks by translating the company strategy into the goals of your team.

However, if you're not one of the lucky ones, communicate your understanding and your expectations effectively by playing to your own communication strengths. Clearly setting expectations goes a long way in the development of effective employee relationships.

Some managers come to the table with some pretty awesome presentation skills in PowerPoint, a tool that can be an exceptional presentation medium. But, if your presentation style is different and you're more comfortable talking it through, or offering a printed outline, that's great. Whatever your style is, go for it! Just be sure that, at the end of the presentation, you offer an opportunity to answer the questions your employees may have. Also, be sure you give them something they can take away from your presentation so they can go back to their desk, define their goals, and get working on achieving the items that you have explicitly outlined for them to achieve over the coming year.

About a week after your presentation, it's important that you circle back to every employee and follow-up with a one-on-one meeting. Address any questions that may have come up after the presentation, and ensure each is clear about the goals and expectations you have set for each team member. Following up is important because not only are you reinforcing your expectations for each member of your team, you are also showing your support for your people and telling them that their goals are important to you.

Ensure Contributions are Clear

We said it before and we'll say it again: Employees need goals...it's what helps them find meaning at work. Even more, employees need to know exactly what you expect of them so that they can meet these expectations or maybe even surpass them! Knowing what a manager expects is the basis for an effective relationship.

And if you did your job exceptionally well as a manager by understanding the company's strategy and translating that into your team's goals, and also giving a heads-up as to what you expect of each member of your team, then aligning the goals of each and every single member of your group shouldn't be that tough. Yes, it takes time, but more importantly, it takes a great deal of conversation.

If you're part of an organization that has a specific goal program, then you will know exactly what is expected of you as a manager. However, if you are not in a company that requires employees to overtly state specific goals, then you will want to ensure that each member of your team is very clear about the specifics of what you expect from them. It's probably a good idea to institute your own team policy and ask each member of your team—after meeting with you—to draft his or her individual goals for your review and approval, just to make sure that everyone—and everything—is clear.

In any event, it is exceptionally important that you spend a great deal of time early in the goal cycle to ensure that your teammates have a thorough understanding of what each member is going to achieve in that year. Simply put, without these types of goals, employees don't know what to do other than what they have done in the past that has been successful for them. However, your number one most important priority during this period is to commit to each of your individual employees to be sure they have and understand their goals. Once you present your team's goals to your employees, follow this process:

1. *Follow-up meeting:* Schedule follow-up meetings with each member of your team one week after presenting your team's goals to gauge their understanding and answer any questions they may have. If you have not done so already, ask them to draft a list of individual goals that you will review with them later.

2. *Individual goal meeting:* Schedule another one-on-one meeting with each member of your team 2-4 days later. Ask each member to bring his or her draft goals to that meeting for your review. During this meeting, be sure to offer specific and actionable feedback on the individual goals shown to you, so that your employee can make revisions and present a final draft within one week.

3. *Team goal meeting:* This is something that few managers do, but it is effective. If you can, schedule a team meeting during which each member of the group presents their goals to the group and relates those goals all the way back to the customer.

Invite employees to offer input into the goals being presented and ask each individual presenter to revise his or her goals for review with you during the final draft meeting.

4. *Final draft meeting:* This is your final opportunity to make any revisions to your employees' goals.

5. *Post team member goals:* Be transparent by asking each of your employees to publicly post their goals for other members of your team, your management hierarchy, and anyone else who you might want to be aware of what your team is working on. Some organizations have the kind of technology that will allow employees to post their goals online and make them available for either a select group of individuals to review or to the entire employee community. Regardless of the type of technology that your organization uses, this type of approach may create a great deal of resistance from your team. They might be shy about publically declaring their intentions, for fear of failing. However, we recommend that you buckle down and get it done so that there is never a question about who is responsible for specific tasks, what they are doing to get the work done, or how your team's work contributes to your organization's overall success. It might be uncomfortable, but you can bet that it will be a hugely successful tactic in the long run.

The best outcome of aligning your employees behind the strategy of the company is to ensure your team is happy, healthy, and productively performing in accordance with company's expectations. Hang on. When you think about it, that's the *second* best outcome from an employee's point of view. The best outcome is that your team members know that the work that they are doing is meaningful and that their contributions have an impact on the company's overall success. It is this point that will serve you as a manager in your pursuit to develop effective relationships.

Once you have your entire team off and running in the right direction, let them own their workspace so they can achieve personal as well as team success. That means you have to take a couple of steps back and allow them to fulfill the tasks they know they need to do but in a way that works well for them. Don't micro manage.

This can be exceptionally tough for anyone, but especially for new managers. It's common to feel that if we know how to do something well, the way we do it is the right way. The truth is that there are hundreds of ways to accomplish a task, and there isn't any one right answer. As a manager, you will experience great success if you just get out of your employees' way and let them work in a way that makes sense for them personally.

There is a great phrase first uttered in management circles: "Trust but verify." Remember it when you need to remind yourself to let your employees have the leeway they need to achieve great success with the task they are assigned, but never be too far away if they should stumble.

Remember, the members of your team are all adults. They have individual responsibilities outside of work that they manage on their own. The good news is that at work they apply the same adult behavior and can manage their own responsibilities there as well.

While they're taking care of their responsibilities, you're free to go off and take care of what you need to get done, too. Of course, you should always check in and verify that progress is being made, but try to do it in a way that isn't overbearing. You're not your employees' parent.

One of the most common ways you can verify progress with your employees is to have a status meeting. Most companies will call this either a "touch base" or a "one-on-one." Call it whatever you want, as long as you use it as an opportunity to pull out the tasks that the employee is assigned to complete and check in with him or her about progress against deliverables.

It's a best practice to check in with your team members about every other week. This way, when you're invited as a manager into quarterly business reviews, you'll have in-depth knowledge of the progress your team is making and you'll be in a better position to outline and verify your team's results when the boss requires a download.

Another way to "trust but verify" is to ask your employees to fill out a written status report. Ask employees what works best for them—a weekly, biweekly, semi-monthly, or monthly written status update would be acceptable—but we think the weekly status update generally works best. A week is long enough to give employees something meaningful to report, but short enough that the reporting isn't going to take up a huge amount of time and effort to pull together.

However, if you were to choose this management tactic, make a note: Allow your team to produce the report as either an e-mail or a Word document. Don't ask for anything as elaborate as a PowerPoint presentation, because it will annoy your team members and accomplish nothing. There is nothing that kills effective employee relationships faster than annoying requests from one's manager.

Some of your employees will want to check in with you on a day-to-day basis, while others will want to work from home and see you every other week during your check-in meetings. Again, there is no right answer, except that you can drive exceptional performance within your team if you and your employees can agree to a working structure that works first and foremost for the employee, but also delivers the hyper-productivity that you seek as a manager.

Some people are more productive in alternative work environments. It may seem counterintuitive that a team member would be more productive working from home with the TV or radio on or being interrupted by a kid or a dog every five minutes, but for some this structure is ideal.

Again, your job here is to "trust but verify" by giving your employees a great deal of room to achieve the type of productivity that you seek from each and every one of them. When you do this right, you'll find your employees will likely not just meet their minimum requirements, but will often exceed your expectations. And when they do, you get to show your manager how your team demonstrates success.

In our experience, it's just when you have your team perfectly aligned and achieving amazing results, that you can expect something to get off schedule or go terribly wrong: Your company's stock crashes, the economy tanks, the company decides to expand its operations globally, your manager leaves, or some other catastrophe befalls you.

In fact, we suggest that you not only expect disaster to strike, that you plan for it. In our experience, managers can only plan for 80 percent of what they think is going to happen. This is a perspective all managers of people should have in the front of their mind as they are thinking about not just aligning their team but keeping them productive over the long haul.

Some business leaders will review their strategy and let you in on their thinking. Others will play it close to the vest and ask you to adjust your business operations, without providing you with the context that you need to understand the decision that they have passed on to you, let alone to change the way that your team is working. But, as a manager, when these types of decisions come down the chain, you can bet that someone has made a decision to change the direction of your organization from here on out.

This is why updating your employees quarterly, regardless of any course corrections that come down the chain, ensures that you are refreshing them about your team's goals, your company's strategy, and their part in it. As a matter of fact, as your team progresses through its list of tasks for the year, you may find that you need to re-adjust your own set of deliverables so that your team is able to achieve its expected results.

To provide your team with the type of update that is necessary here—use the same approach you would use when you present the company's strategy, your organization's business priorities, and your team's goals to your employees. This update will help your employees understand which of their team goals have been changed and how it will affect them. You can simply update that presentation, but point out the changes explicitly so they understand what's changing and what's not, as well as their role in all of it.

You may find these update meetings can result in a high degree of employee frustration. Think of it from their perspective; you're knee-deep in a very complex project, you been working nights and weekends, missing birthdays, and burning the proverbial candle at both ends. Then, someone comes along and tells you that what you been working so diligently on just isn't all that important anymore. That's enough to send any stressed-out, over-worked but dedicated employee over the edge.

So as you develop your updated presentation, be sure that you also give credit to any employees who have been working hard on priorities that no longer exist or have been significantly modified. As a matter of fact, it is a very good idea to meet with these employees one on one before you present any updates to the rest of the team so they feel you are genuinely aware and appreciative of their contributions and their hard work, as well as their emotional commitment to the project that you're terminating. By having these meetings you're showing your respect for them as human beings, rather than viewing them as merely cogs in a wheel that is no longer required.
The crux here remains unchanged. As business priorities change—and they will—employees and their goals need to change with them.

As a result, to be successful in your role as a manager of people, you have to become exceptionally good at getting comfortable very quickly with shifting business priorities, and giving these updates to your team in a way that gets them excited about the new direction you're asking them to take. Acknowledge where you've been and then focus your team on where you're going, while highlighting the benefits for the employee, the team, your organization, and your company altogether.

When you do this right, your team will be a powerhouse of performance. Not only will they be able to focus on the types of projects that are important to them, you will not lose any time in the team's quest to achieve what is being asked of them.

Overcome the Inevitable

Here's the biggest secret that you already know: Being a manager means overcoming more obstacles then you could ever imagine—every day! That's right; a manager's job is to remove roadblocks. Effective relationship building includes helping someone succeed in their role; and the obstacles at any company can stop someone dead in their tacks. So, if you think being a manager is an easy path to fame and fortune, we hate to be the ones that have to break to you that it's just not. It is, however, a great way to build relationships with people that extend beyond the work place and across time.

While overcoming obstacles is only one part of the job, it's the most critical work you'll do. Ironically, most companies today indicate that removing obstacles is a relatively small part of a manager's role, in comparison to being a company cheerleader for your team and pushing your team for results. But, it's those ubiquitous obstacles that prevent good communication and productivity in the first place and can all but shut down the work your team is focused on delivering.

To learn how to overcome obstacles, you'll need to get very clear on the different types of challenges you will face as a manager, prepare well in advance of facing obstacles, and become exceptionally good at the art of persuasive communications.

You can get a jump on preparing to face obstacles by taking some time to think through all of the obstacles you've confronted as an employee and create a comprehensive list. Make sure your list include obstacles in the following areas: budget, legal, human resources, the people on your team, the people in your management hierarchy, etc. We stopped there, but the list of types of obstacles could clearly go further.

Expect to face all of these at one time or another and often simultaneously.

If obstacles cripple you, we highly recommend you get out of your management role, right now. Seriously, it's not for you. Don't walk to your manager's office, cube, or desk to have that discussion—run! There is no time like the present to get yourself out of the wrong job... before it is just too late. Obstacles will be ever-present in your life, but even more so when you step into the manager's role. The good news is you don't have to react to these obstacles in a way that is overly emotional, as described in earlier chapters. You don't have to take on these obstacles as a personal attack against yourself.

Obstacles are tough to deal with; they block progress and make life difficult. Throughout the rest of this chapter, we offer you some big ideas on how to challenge yourself to overcome obstacles. This is tough stuff, but we try our best to make it at least a little fun to work through. So go ahead: Challenge yourself to overcome the biggest obstacles standing between you and success!

The best approach to overcoming obstacles as a manager is to know what you can and cannot influence, change, or otherwise control. If you can't control something, it's best to not even try. Trying to change something that you have no control over creates frustration and there is no reason to become frustrated in your role as a manager. Although not typically offered up to managers to help them to understand how to overcome obstacles in the workplace, the Serenity Prayer, written by Reinhold Niebuhr, is one from which you can draw a great deal of wisdom.

"God, grant me the serenity
To accept the things I cannot change,
Courage to change the things I can,
and wisdom to know the difference."

The poem itself is one from which all managers can benefit—regardless of your spiritual beliefs. The core meaning is to simply know what you are in control of and what you are not. This way, you don't waste your time and energy trying to overcome obstacles that just can't be overcome. This will result in giving you more time to be with your family and friends and to be focused on those things that are important to you. Essentially, you'll be happier, healthier, and more productive because you won't be weighed down by situations that you cannot affect. You will also experience a work-life balance that is right for you. Most importantly, you will be better able to tell your employees what is possible, which leads to clear expectations and results in more effective relationships.

Proactively Develop a Staffing Model

Every manager at some point in his or her managerial career will run up against the one unifying problem that all managers have — staff! As a manager, you play the middle role. On one hand, your leadership team expects you to get a number of different activities done with a limited budget. On the other hand, your people are overworked and frustrated because they need help to accomplish what is expected of them. So what you do? We believe there are four activities you can do to help overcome staffing issues:

1. Develop a staffing model to achieve the results that your manager seeks from your team.

2. Work with your manager to set a clear set of specific priorities.

3. Create a plan to ask for the budget you need.

4. Get budget to hire temporary staff or independent contractors to fill the gap.

Developing a staffing model is difficult if you've never done it before. And even if you have, the depth of analysis that you and your team will go through to develop a model that meets the needs of the business is a treacherous activity, at best. However, if your business requires deep analysis to get approval just to get additional help, then this is an activity you should get exceedingly good at. You cannot just make the case for headcount based on your experience and best guess. You will need to tell the specific story as to how that headcount will be deployed and the exact results to be achieved by your team in exchange for investing in a new employee joining your team.

But hey, this doesn't have to be too scary. The good news is that there are some big ideas that can help you right here in this book. And if this doesn't work, check in with your mentor or HR Business Partner to get company-specific advice. You can do it! We have faith!

There are at least 100 different processes that you can go through to get to your staffing model. We will focus on the one that seems to have worked best for us in the past.

Below, you will find a long and detailed step-by-step process to creating a staffing model. Don't let your eyes glaze over while you read it, but do spend some time with this because having a process to create your staffing model can make or break your success. So, while you might find it a little boring and dry, power through so that you have this tool in your managerial toolbox.

To illustrate what happens in each step, we've created an example to show you how it works. In this case, the example helps demonstrate how much time it takes to close the books. While closing the books is not all that much fun for anyone, even accountants, it sure does work well to show you how to move through this process. But rather than focusing in on the details of closing the books, give yourself a break and just enjoy the story.

Headcount Preparation Process	
Step-by-Step Process	Description
1. List Each Goal	Looking back to the chapter on strategic alignment, remember how you strategically aligned the goals of your team to the strategic priorities of your company? As a manager, you will need to be very good at strategic alignment to make the best case for hiring staff. It's one of the most important roles you will play. And, if you work through this activity in a way that is both meaningful and relevant, you are already halfway through the process of developing your staffing model. So for this example, imagine that "closing the books on time each month" is your team's responsibility to achieving the strategy.

2. Detail the Tasks	Each goal you outline will likely have a large number of tasks that need to be completed. Examine each specific task to determine the amount of time that it takes to complete. In this case, list out each task that needs to be completed to "close the books on time each month." You would probably want to include training, staff meetings, running reports, auditing cash flow, reviewing delinquent accounts, etc.
3. Identify Obstacles	Once you have created your list of tasks, identify the obstacles that stand in the way of that task being completed. So in this case, you might list sick employees, IT systems-wide outage, paper jams, etc.
4. Estimate Time	Now that you know both the specific task that your team is responsible for completing, as well as the amount of time you need to overcome obstacles that exist in any job, add those numbers together to determine the amount of time it takes to complete a task each month. Here's a hint: Even when you list out every obstacle you can think of, something will come up that stands in your way. So, be sure to add on at least 20% more time to ensure that you are covered when the

	inevitable strikes. And for recurring tasks, be sure you multiply whatever unit of time it takes to complete the task by the number of times the task has to be completed. For example, if each month you have to close your books, and there are 10 steps in that task and each takes one hour, then each month you are spending 10 hours to close the books. Multiply 10 hours times 12 months, and you get a total of 144 hours a year for your team to achieve this goal, which contributes to the company's strategy.

Now, repeat this activity for each goal, then add up the total number of hours that your team needs to complete the tasks you've signed up to deliver in any given year.

You can use the below table to document the tasks that line up under your goal, identify the obstacles, and estimate the time that is required to complete each task. Then, add up all of your estimated time into one big number and that tells you how long it will take you and your team to achieve the goal.

Goal:			
	Task 1:	*Task 2:*	*Task 3:*
Details			
Obstacles			
Estimated Time to Complete			
Total Time			

Now we are going in deep to the next phase of the process, which is to figure out how many people you need to complete the goals your team is signed up to deliver. So, based on the number of goals you have, and the subsequent tasks, estimate the number of hours you need to achieve the direction your team has set out to achieve in any given year.

So let's imagine then that this finance manager, the person responsible for managing the team that closes the books, has gone through this exercise and detailed not just the tasks and obstacles associated with this goal, but the tasks and obstacles associated with all of the goals his or her team is responsible for achieving. From there, this manager added up all of the time estimates and discovered that to complete all of the goals, it would take 5,467 hours. So then, how many people are needed to complete the work? Now, that's an easy one.

But first, one little note that if missed can completely throw off your staffing model calculation. The definition of "full-time" varies from country to country. In the U.S., for example, 40 hours per work is considered full time. However, in France, 35 hours per work is considered full time. If you are a manager who has employees in just one country, what comes next will be exceptionally easy for you. However, if you are a manager who has employees in multiple countries, be sure you take the appropriate full-time hours into account.

In the below example, we'll make it easy and use the standard, U.S. 40-hour work week, which is equal to 2,080 hours per year. To calculate the total number of employees you will need to complete your goals, simply divide the total time by 2,080.

Calculate Headcount		
Total Time	/2,080	= Number of Full-time Employees
Ex: 5,467	/2,080	=2.6

So, as you can see here, this manager needs at least two full-time employees and one part-time employee.

Although this is a lot of math and not a lot about the actual work your group will be doing, it is the type of detailed planning that is exceptionally important when you go to ask your manager for additional headcount. In fact, it will likely blow his or her mind that you were so thoughtful and diligent about how you would like to spend the company's money.

If you go through this model or one similar to it, you'll be able to speak specifically to any question that your manager has about your team. This includes your team's ability to achieve its goals for the type of work that it is tasked with doing and how much time it takes to do it. There are very few people in management who ever go through the hard work of figuring out what their headcount should be; rather, they tend to ask based on emotion and in response to the fact that their team is burned out and over-worked.

However, if you go to your manager with this type of model and ask for what you need, your manager can then either say, "Yes let's go ahead and hire people so you can continue to achieve the good work you are achieving" or "No, we just can't afford to hire anyone else." If the latter is the answer; then it is incumbent upon you to tell your manager that you need to reduce the tasks that your team is being asked to achieve. There is a great legal reason for doing this.

Following on with the above example: In the United States, the work week is legally defined as 40 hours per week. Regular full-time jobs can only be designed to max out at 40 hours a week. And, if your company is requiring that a specific job is more than 40 hours a week, then there are legal ramifications that should be presented to your legal team to resolve with your manager and HR. Be sure you know the laws of your country, state, and local government so that you are able to best plan the right type of work environment for your people. A work environment that is happy, healthy, and productive also respects its employees as individuals in this world. That's where the humanity in all of this comes in and that's why planning is so critically important when you are considering the obstacles of staffing.

So, here's where it all gets a little corporate-y… so bear with us.

Generally speaking, if your manager is one who agrees with you and is supportive in getting the additional headcount to achieve the goals of your team, then you need to review your staffing model and determine if the headcount you need is needed for more than one year, or if these tasks your team needs to complete are temporary. If temporary, you may need someone on a contract basis for anywhere between six months to one year. In any regard, it is critically important when you present your headcount needs and staffing model to your manager that you point out to him or her the cost savings that can be achieved by hiring either temps or contractors.

Know the Numbers

Your company is likely in the business of making money rather than spending it. As a manager, you can then expect to be faced with financial obstacles at every turn. Ironically, this concept of not spending money is often in conflict with what the company is asking of you as a manager. You have to spend money to make money, right?

When it comes to financial obstacles, the biggest challenge you'll likely have to overcome is creating a projected budget or managing your annual budget or both. In some organizations, the annual budget is basically managed at the top, which reduces the manager's ability to make wise decisions in the management of his or her team, since there's minimal insight into the financials behind the work the company is asking the team to complete. More often, as a manager, you'll be asked to take on a new project, but you will not always be provided with additional budget to get it done. Be very clear that when these new projects are presented to you, you ask what budget and resources are available to complete the project. Without the financial resources you need, your team will not succeed; and when success isn't evident on your team, effective relationships will soon sour.

Often these projects are inserted last-minute and go above and beyond the tasks that were agreed to for the year. This is why you budgeted an extra 20% more time in your staffing plan, as we discussed earlier in this chapter, to make up the difference. If you outright ask for the budget and resources, your manager may be ticked off by your approach. However, as a manager, it is your responsibility to ensure that you have everything necessary to create success for your team, and part of that is being savvy enough to plan ahead for this type road-bock.

By creating the headcount plan as described in the previous section, you'll already have the majority of the costs that you will need to identify for an annual budget. That's because together, salary and benefits are the largest budget items on any annual budget for any company in the world. So, to get to your annual budget, you just need to go back and look at the tasks that you've already determined the headcount for and determine the exact level, skills, and responsibilities of the roles you would need to hire to successfully complete those tasks.

From there, work with a compensation analyst at your organization to determine the exact salary for the year, cost of benefits, and any other related labor costs that you need to be aware of. Then, look over the tasks that you have listed and identify the hard costs, meaning the materials that you will need to buy. Although it may seem odd, if you need to hire a temp or an independent contractor, those costs would be added in too—separate from headcount.

All these variable costs need to be considered to get the job done. Finally, determine which months you need to hire headcount or temporary workers, and calculate the months in which you would need to buy materials to complete the work. Once you have your headcount, temporary and contract labor, and material costs laid out along the task-specific timeline, you will have your annual budget very clearly identified.

Be Creative to Get the Job Done

When you add up the obstacles of not having enough staff or money to get the job done, many managers would think to throw in the towel. Lack of resources, overworked people, and a tight deadline can be enough to make even the most seasoned managers break. But not you! You're a crafty manager. You'll get the job done for sure, and you'll do it without burning your people out.

If you're burdened with limited staff and no money, and a boss who insists that you get the job done anyway, the best thing you can do is to step back from the project and start to see the big picture of what your work means to your company. If it indeed the project is important to your company's success, then it's highly likely that other groups outside of your department have a stake in the outcome of your team's work. So, it might mean they have staff, budget, or other types of resources that can be contributed to your team to help you get the job done.

To get the type of resources you need from other teams, you first have to either make your project so critical to the company's success that they have no choice but to invest in it, or stroke their delicate egos so that they are willing to invest in a portion of the work, likely a portion that is beneficial to both teams. To do that, you again need to dig deeply into the goals you are being asked to complete. Effectively working with other teams is always based in the goals you share.

To do just that, you are going to need a game plan. First and foremost, you need to determine if your manager will support you in going to other departments to ask for help, resources, or staff to achieve the goals that your teams share. If you just don't think your manager would be supportive of that approach, you might want to go ahead and do it and ask for forgiveness after the project has been completed successfully. Of course, the ideal situation would be that your manager fully supports your request of asking another department for help and joins you on your crusade to secure new resources. You already know which situation is more likely in your company.

Regardless of your manager's level of support, asking other teams for their resources is the final straw in terms of being able to achieve the goals your team is tasked. So, get very clear about the type of work your team can do with its current headcount and budget, and strictly prioritize those tasks that are completely in line with the goals that are most critical to your team's success. Then, using the below list of questions to get started, create your game plan.

Is this approach a little risky? Sure it is. The outcome of this type of scenario is rarely known at the onset of your crusade. However, as a manager, it is your responsibility to take calculated risks; and, if your team is not wealthy enough or provided the right resources, then as a manager you need to be crafty in securing the means to accomplish your goals. Bottom-line: If you can't get the support you need, you might as well go out and secure it on your own.

Develop your strategy and target those executives, departments, or teams that have a stake in your team's success. Ask yourself the following questions to devise your master plan:

- Which executives in my department will be directly impacted by this work?
- If this work does not get completed in this year, who will scream the loudest?
- If we only complete a part of this work, which department would be able to pick it up and finish the job?
- How much money do we need from a different team to complete this work?
- If I ask another department to fund the headcount to complete these tasks, which department has the biggest discretionary budget?
- How can I make this project important to a team with a large discretionary budget?

Once you have the answers to these questions, as well as a few others that you would likely think up on your own, develop a proposal that is 100% focused on the other department from which you seek resources. You do not need to focus so much on what you can or cannot achieve with the resources you don't have today. Focus on the successful outcome that your target department will have if they agree to pony up money, time, headcount, or resources in some way that will achieve the final result. Then, when the goal has been successfully achieved, be sure to point to that team as the reason it was such a success, while being sure to talk to your team about all of their work and your reasoning for doing so "behind the scenes."

Stand Up to the Legal Department

If you can make it through all the budgetary and staffing obstacles that will likely be in your way, the great big sand pit you have yet to encounter is likely the notorious Legal department.

Yup, lawyers being lawyers can completely block you from being able to achieve the goals the company has asked you to achieve. The bad news is that lawyers tend to only focus on risk management, rather than corporate achievement. It's in their nature—their job is to protect the company, but expect that situation going in. A lawyer will try to tell you you're wrong even if you know you're right. Why? Because they just want to avoid any possible litigation that may result from one minor error. Do mistakes happen? Absolutely! But that's why we have attorneys—to help us out of those sticky situations.

So if you have to go to Legal to get an initiative agreed upon, go in with the following set of objectives:

- *Provide your business reasons*: Before you even step foot into your general counsel's office, be sure you have your business reasons not just lined up and ready to present to the attorney, but also completely agreed to by your leadership. This is where your manager is required to ensure the business reasons you have are totally aligned with the business strategy of your company. Have three solid business reasons for why your proposal is critical to the success of the company. This is a best practice in any type of decision-making, though particularly when you go into your corporate attorney's office. If even one of the reasons is a little bit shaky, rewrite it before you present it, because a good attorney will cut right through the bull and point out every minute flaw. Take the time to do this right; a well-written and thoughtful proposal will impress even the toughest lawyers.

- *Prove the return on investment*: Even though most lawyers are not accountants, they do get a lot of training in financials, particular those attorneys who support corporations. So, if your three business decisions are unflappable, it's likely that the attorney will jump right into the financials that go along with your business strategy and start to tear those numbers apart, decimal point by decimal point. At this stage, your role is to provide sound projections for the financial outcome if these business strategies were to be implemented by the company. Bring your budget, to prove your point, and also show your thorough analysis of the scenario for which you are seeking approval.

- *Answer any risks upfront:* As previously stated, most attorneys only look to find the risk that is associated with your proposal. As soon as they sniff out the risk, they have a reason to block you from getting what you want. But law is not the world of business nor is it the world of humanity. As a manager of people and of a function in any business, you need to be comfortable taking risks. We are speaking of calculated risks and not thoughtless, irresponsible risks. When you meet with the attorney, point out the potential risks you see with the scenario that you're proposing, but also point out how you plan to mitigate those risks so the company is not challenged in a court of law. This will show you are doing your job of always keeping the company in mind, even from a legal standpoint.

- *Negotiate for an agreeable outcome:* No one expects you to have a deep understanding of the law, which is why companies hire attorneys. That is their skill set. Your skill set is completely aligned to the function that you are running for the organization. Let the attorney be an attorney and point out all of the potential risks that he or she identifies with your proposal. And, as the business strategist, be on your toes and fully able to respond to these legal scenarios that the attorney is pointing out. You would likely want to come up with risk scenarios before you even enter your legal counsel's office. Why? So you are ready to negotiate. It may mean that you get to do what you want, even in a risky situation. But, under the guidance of your legal counsel, you at least know the full opportunity for risk that you're putting the company in with your proposal.

Now, this is where it gets tricky. If your company's legal counsel feels there is too great a risk to the company involved with your proposal—the very proposal that has complete and utter support all the way up your management chain—he or she may insist that you do not pursue that proposal in part or at all. There may be very good reasons for this, all of which the attorney will explain to you during your meeting. And, if the flaws in your plan are so great that they put the company at risk in ways that it would be unable to recover from, then it is likely that your project will never see the light of day.

When employees work hard on a project that is killed in the final phases, it can often be a crushing blow. Too many blows, and trust in you as their manager erodes. Without trust, effective relationships aren't possible.

So, it is in your best interest to be very well prepared before you step foot into the Legal department.

If your attorney does put the kibosh on your project or hacked it to unrecognizable pieces, it is time to take your proposal back up the chain to your manager. It was your manager, if you remember, who tasked you with this project in the first place. This is your last chance to keep the project alive and demonstrate results to your team.

Since you, your manager, and your legal counsel are all working for the same company, you should be able to find some common ground that will get your initiative moving. Take your proposal back to your manager, along with the risks the attorney cited, to ensure that he or she understands the legal counsel, and then set up the meeting for the three of you to talk. During that meeting, play a neutral stance where you allow the attorney and your manager to work it out or dissolve the project entirely.

Manage Your Manager As Much As You Manage Your Employees

Unexpectedly, your own manager may be the biggest obstacle that you may ever have to overcome in the workplace. It seems entirely counter to the productivity of your team that you would have to convince your manager to make a change or implement a new program or strategy.

Most people tend to be focused on what they need to achieve in a way they know how to achieve it, rather than looking outside of the box to see if there's a better way to get the work done. As the manager of your team, you can be of great service to these individuals if you are able to allow their ideas to flow forward to you, which will then make their work even better. After all, it is the people who put their hands on the work being done that typically understand the best ways to accomplish it. So, when these ideas flow to you, you will need to float them up the chain to get them implemented in a way that makes sense for the business.

Selling your idea to your manager will take a great deal of persuasive dialogue. You will need to have a system that you can use to win over your manager—a model of sorts. And, like all good persuasive arguments, it is highly important to synthesize information from a number of different sources so you can develop a model that's going to work well for you when you present to your manager.

And, at the end of the day, you need a model that can help you move through the process fluidly. All types of persuasive models start with the obvious, which is to describe the current situation that you are dealing with. In this part of your persuasive dialogue with your manager, your presentation needs to sell the new program. Spell out these simple high-level statements of the current situation, and spell out all of the obstacles that the current situation creates. Also, bring relevant metrics into this meeting. If the numbers tell an interesting story, use those numbers to make dollars and sense of the issue that you are attempting to solve.

The next step in persuading your manager is to outline the desired state. In other words, if your manager were to agree to your change, define for your manager exactly what the situation will look like after implementation has occurred. Again, you will want to use specific metrics to make your point. For example, if you are recommending a process change and the current process costs you $100 and the process that you seek to implement will cost you $50 and take half the time, then your persuasive argument is very clear, right? Well, not always. Often it will take at least three solid business reasons to change anyone's thinking in the workplace. So with your desired state, be sure to clearly articulate the three business reasons that support the change. This will help you create a better outcome after the changes are implemented.

It is important when you are attempting to persuade someone to do something that you give them a call-to-action. Call-to-action is a commonly used phrase that asks a practical question while evoking an emotional response. Your call -to-action must be passionate, easy to implement, and something that your manager can just say "yes" to. While your manager will be resistant to change, it is your job to keep him or her from saying "no."

Remember, your manager may or may not need to know all the details of the change you are recommending, but you want to get him or her closer to saying "yes." So with this in mind, make sure you have your sales thinking cap on to help you overcome your manager's objections and move him or her to a state of mind of complete agreement with you, with no hesitations about your proposal.

Once your initiative is successful, it is exceptionally important that you go back to your manager and present the success of the program to him or her. Point out how the strategy, or the new way of doing business, was a success because of the change you recommended and oversaw. Take this opportunity to build your own personal credibility and point out your team's expertise on fulfilling the work. This proves the fact that you are doing what's right on behalf of the business.

Overcoming obstacles is frustrating and takes a great deal of hard work, persuasion, and attention to detail.

As a manager of people, as a manager of function, and as a manager of the business, you have a great deal of work each and every day just overcoming roadblocks. Whether it be budget, headcount, or just getting a simple "yes," overcoming obstacles on a day-to-day basis can be exceptionally taxing.

However, you are the leader of your team. That means what you have to do each and every day is to clear a path so your team can efficiently move forward to achieve the results it seeks. That also means that you may need to delegate some of your day-to-day, hands-on work so you have time to meet with people outside of your department to grease the wheels and ensure what your team is working towards is attainable. Sometimes this part of your job will be challenging and other times you'll find it a pleasure. The lesson here is to focus on removing these obstacles so your team's success can proliferate throughout the organization and be an inspiration for others to see what can be achieved within your company.

You can do this! No obstacle is too great to overcome when you are making the right business decisions for your company. Be aware of all the challenges and obstacles standing in your way. But, do yourself a favor and have all of your prep-work done up-front so you always know the right answer. Your thoughtful preparation can counter any argument you encounter, regardless of who's presenting it. Being prepared can leave you with a feeling of massive achievement, even in those times when you get shot down.

Get Cozy with Change

There is one thing that will never change about your role as a manager, and that's the fact that you'll have to deal with change almost constantly. Ironically, dealing with change may be the most constant part of your managerial experience; and when you manage change exceptionally well, you will be able to maintain effective employee relationships even in the face of constantly changing priorities.

The pace of change is often a reflection of the speed at which the company is growing. If you work for a start-up company, you can bet that no two days will ever be the same. Even larger and established businesses change often, though the larger a company is, the more likely it is to have policies that govern most of its business practices. But even for big corporations, just like start-ups, as soon as there is a blip in the matrix, the systems, policies and procedures will all quickly adjust to support the business change, sometimes without anyone knowing that the change occurred.

In your role as a manager, you will be asked to help employees through the change, even when no one has helped you to move through the change. So, it is important that you ask the right questions and set yourself up to succeed with your people.

To do so, you need to know the elements of a formal change management plan. Although there are hundreds of change models in the world from which a plan can be created, most will use the following core elements:

1. *Today's current state:* The current state is exactly what it sounds like—the situation today.

2. *Tomorrow's ideal state:* The ideal state is the situation that will exist after the change is implemented and fully adopted.

3. *The delta details:* The delta is the difference between the two. This is one of the most often overlooked elements of a change management plan because most employees are rarely trained to be managers of change and they tend to focus on the differences between the current and ideal state, and not on what employees need to do to get to the ideal state. However, some employees hold on tightly to history, while others will quickly adopt the ideal state situation. You would be wise to spend time honoring the current state and helping employees to bridge the gap by being very clear about the delta and the reasons that the idea state is better.

4. *Communication:* The best change management plans include a communication plan that goes beyond one e-mail to all employees announcing the change. As a manager, you should look to your leaders to provide you with communications tools and resources to help you deliver the change message, as well as get comfortable with the change yourself. Communications tools and resources can come in a variety of forms, but often include e-mail templates, meeting templates, Q&A documents, and the like.

5. *Training:* Not every company will be large enough to have a full-fledged training team that is entirely committed to change. As a matter of fact, only the largest of the large companies will offer this support to help employees through a change. And as a manager, you will likely not

have a lot of extra time to develop your own training program. However, you should be sure to take at least ten minutes during your team meeting to walk your team through a new process or procedure. Think of this type of investment in time as a mini-training program, one that will have significant return on your investment when you show that you are committed to getting to the ideal state.

6. *Rewards:* It is a rare day that you will see a company reward anything other than negative behavior when it comes to change. As a matter of fact, spending so much time focused on negative behavior is one of the great corporate mysteries. As a manager, however, you can spend your time rewarding those employees who move through the change to the ideal state with recognition and other special treats that reinforce the behaviors you seek from your team. Reward them publically so that everyone on your team knows what is important to you.

7. *Reinforcement:* People don't like change. It is often said that it takes 28 days to change a behavior. You can change your behavior and so can the members of your team; and to do that, just to reward them until the change is made and until you are confident that it is fully adopted.

Since change management is something that you will only experience when it comes up, it is best to understand exactly what the plan looks like ahead of time. As such, below we have set up a high-level plan that illustrates a non-business change—weight loss. We are using weight loss because it is something everyone has heard of at least once and would likely have some level of knowledge about before picking up this book. So, here it goes: The change is to lose ten pounds.

Change Management Example	
Today's Current State:	I weigh 185 pounds.
Tomorrow's Ideal State:	I weigh ten pounds less.
The Delta Details:	1. Lose ten pounds. 2. Don't eat ice cream. 3. Exercise at least three times each week. 4. Ask friends to support my goal.
Communication:	1. Weigh myself each day to chart progress, post on wall next to scale. 2. Write note on fridge reminding me to leave the ice cream alone. 3. Contact trainer to schedule three appointments per week. 4. Invite friends, via e-mail, to a healthy meal at my house, advise of my goal and ask them for their support.
Training:	1. Work out at a gym with a trainer at least three times each week for a minimum of one hour. 2. Walk to work each day.
Rewards:	1. Reach my goal weight, get a tattoo. 2. Reach goal weight, buy new shoes.

Reinforcement:	1. Set reminder in my smart phone to eat the right foods once I have reached my goal weight. 2. Weigh myself each week to ensure I remind myself of my ideal weight goals.

Although the example doesn't have anything to do with a business situation, it does have everything to do with a human situation and being a human first and foremost is the most important action you can take as a manager. It also illustrates how to plan at a very high level. In business, you will want to go much deeper; however, when you apply a change management plan, you can get your team comfortable with the change faster, which means that you will be able to produce bigger, better results much faster.

Plan to Quickly Adapt

As a manager, change is an inevitability that you should come to expect as a part of working at any company. Businesses change each and every day and often at the most inconvenient times. More often than not, you will not be a part of the process that initiates the change, but you will certainly be responsible for accomplishing the new set of priorities. Whatever changes come your way, you must deal with them as a manager. The truth is you need to be able to negotiate change realistically and consistently across any type of scenario.

Over the course of a year, your team's goals will take minor course corrections, or may change completely as a result of a change in the company's strategy to meet the needs of its customers. When this happens, ask a lot of questions to understand how the changes impact your team's goals. Get clear about your team's ability to achieve its goals in light of these changes with the resources you have, the budget you have been allocated, and the timeline that has been imposed.

Although there is an exhaustive list of questions that you can ask a manager about any type of change that comes down the pipe, below is a simple list that will get you started:

- What do you want my team to start doing?
- What do you want my team to stop doing so that we can get this priority completed?
- What do you want my team to do less of so that we can put more time to this new priority?
- What do you want my team to do more of that may help us complete this priority faster?
- Will I receive additional headcount to complete this priority?
- What is the budget for this priority?
- When do you need this priority completed?

Based on the answers that your manager provides to you, you may have to reexamine your goals. If these changes turn into one or more massive projects that suck all of your budget headcount and resources, then it's likely that you will have to increase your budget and allocate much greater resources to your team then you would have planned for the year. If that's the case, don't be shy. Again, your manager will likely want to get as much productivity out of your team with as little investment possible. If this sounds like your manager, it means there will be a great deal of burnout not just for you, but for your overworked team as well. It's your job to play the middleman between your team and company leaders and help avoid burnout and attrition for the company at large.

It's also your role to take that new priority and develop a staffing plan, which we described earlier. All changes require reworking your headcount to ensure success. First, examine the timeline in which the project is supposed to be completed and decide how much people time the project will take. Then, determine the headcount you need to successfully complete the project. Finally, determine the expenses and material costs that arise from this type of a project. With all that information in hand, you are ready to meet with your manager.

Now, that plan may include the fact that you will not be able to achieve other goals that your team had already signed up for. Your aim now is to get your manager's support in removing those goals from your list for the year. Don't let your manager get away with adding on more and more projects to your plate without giving you what you need to get them done. If your manager's doing that, he or she is truly setting you up for failure.

Make Recognition Your Key to Success

In order to drive high performance on your team, employees must find the work meaningful. And to help them understand that their work is indeed meaningful, offer them something that puts the spotlight on their success—recognition!

Rewarding behavior with a sincere recognition of the employee's contributions—especially those employees who go above and beyond what is expected of them—is something that you should consider to be an important part of your duties as a manger. Your employees will want to know that you not only acknowledge that they are doing a terrific job, but also that you are willing to publicly give them credit for the work they have done. Recognition is the secret sauce in the development of effective employee relationships.

The types of rewards that companies offer for exceptional performance vary pretty widely—from a pat on the back to a substantial bonus. Some companies acknowledge the contributions of their employees through special events. For sales teams, high performers are often provided with some kind of "all expenses paid" resort vacation in recognition of their exceptional sales performances. That kind of reward is rare for those non-sales employees, who usually receive large bonuses instead.

However, if you are a manager in an organization that does not have a special rewards or recognition program, take the time to understand what's important to your employees. Then, recognize them in the ways that are meaningful to them as they contribute positive results to your team's overall goals.

How do you do that? By getting to know your employees exceedingly well. One way to find out what's important to your employees when it comes to recognition is to develop a set of questions you can use to either interview your employees or ask them to answer by e-mail. Then file away those responses until the employee makes an exceptional contribution. This is the time to pull that form out and figure out which type of reward would be most appropriate for that employee. It is critically important in those companies that do not offer rewards or recognition programs to provide meaningful rewards that don't cost the company anything. You might be willing to spend a little money out-of-pocket to fuel performance, but most of us tend to not go with that approach.

Humans are social beings and want to know each other personally. It just makes everything better. The set of questions to ask your employees will vary from manager to manager and company to company. However, here's our list that you can use to get yourself started in the development of your own personal template—one that will be customized to your team's needs. You can provide the chart below to your employees to complete, which give you a list of rewards that are meaningful to them.

Employee Rewards Survey	
What type of music do you like?	
Who is your favorite author?	
If you could take in all expenses paid trip anywhere in the world where would it be? And why?	
What is your favorite restaurant?	
On a scale of 1 to 10, how important is public recognition for you?	
How important is paid time off to you?	
When you spend time away from work, what you enjoy doing most? And with whom?	

While this is a short list of questions, it should result in important and revealing answers that will help you get to know your employees a little better—as people, not just as cogs in the machine you're trying to create.

Informal Rewards Strategy

If you choose to elicit answers to these questions in an informal meeting or conversation down the road, when you give your employee a reward based on his or her answers, you'll find your employees see that you know who they are as a person. Just like you, all human beings feel that personal relationships are important, and getting to know your team individually will prove how much you care about your relationship with that person.

Formal Rewards Strategy

The most common type of reward program is a formalized bonus program. These bonuses may come in three ways:

1. *A "spot bonus"*: Something that a manager would reward employees with outside of the performance review process that would result in an annual or semiannual bonus.

2. *An annual or semiannual bonus*: Results from the work that an employee does, as measured by a performance review.

3. *A long-term incentive:* Based on performance criteria, could result in a long-term cash bonus or even stock awards.

Don't Get Stuck in the Peanut Butter

The most important rule that you can apply to your decisions about who gets a bonus and how much that bonus would be is this: Never "peanut butter" rewards. Imagine yourself with a great big scoop of peanut butter on a knife. You smoothly and evenly spread that peanut butter over the entire surface of a slice of bread. The peanut butter is the rewards program and the bread represents your team. By "peanut buttering," you have evenly provided the same type of reward and recognition to every single person on your team. This is not the way to manage a rewards program for a team made up of unique individuals. Make it a priority that you will not do this.

As a manager, your role is to drive productivity across your entire group. And as we already explained, the most effective way to drive productivity is to offer rewards to individuals on your team for the exceptional types of contributions that they make your organization.

Instead of "peanut-buttering" the rewards you distribute, concentrate those rewards on those people who are delivering the highest performance for your team. That means not every member of your team will receive the same type of reward or recognition. As a matter of fact, only those employees who are performing at the highest levels will receive the largest rewards, while those employees who are far below the line of what's acceptable would likely receive a very little reward, if any at all.

As a manager, you're responsible for making these types of recommendations for employee rewards to your own management chain. If you make reward recommendations that are not based on merit, but just based on showing up to the office and working, then they will likely view your managerial decision-making as flawed. That would be bad. You don't want that. Rather, as you make rewards recommendations, make them based on the merits of the contribution that the individual employee has provided to your team's overall success. When you do that, you'll easily be able to retain the employees who are the best for your team and the company, while also clearly focusing on those employees who need to either improve their performance, or whose skills would be better suited to another department.

If your goal truly is to build effective relationships, double down on your efforts to reward employees for both big and small accomplishments. When you do this well and with sincerity, you'll find that your team will not only respect you as their manager and leader, they will be there to support you through tough business times with a great deal of enthusiasm and love. Why? Because you helped them see that their work is important and you rewarded them for doing it. Who doesn't love that?

Prioritize Your Personal Wellbeing

Being a manager means that you are in a helping profession; still who is there to help you when you need it? Well, probably you. That just seems to be the way of the world. Which means you mostly focus on everyone else but you. And in order to help others succeed, it is critically important that you take care of yourself first. Otherwise, there will be nothing left to give to your team. And if there is nothing left for your team, then there is no possible way to have effective employee relationships.

Most people who are in managerial roles never consider focusing on their own wellbeing and rarely recognize the impact personal wellbeing has on relationships—until it is too late. As a manager, you simply must take time out to take care of yourself, even if it feels unnatural or as if you are wasting time or being selfish. Why? Because if you are not happy and healthy, then how can you hope to be a positive and productive leader for others? You must be willing to help yourself and commit to your own personal wellbeing before you can have a highly effective relationship with your employees.

Taking care of yourself is often overlooked in the hustle and bustle of a busy workday, but you owe it to yourself to separate from work however briefly. Make "you time" a priority: Go get a massage, meditate, work out, enjoy the sunshine, have lunch with friends, barbeque with family, or anything that you enjoy doing. It's totally up to you to decide the best part of "you time." It's all about you!

Even the busiest managers have found ways to dedicate time for themselves, and so will you. The best way to ensure that you are getting time to recharge your batteries is to schedule it, just like you would a vacation. It's important to schedule your "you time" each and every day, in order to take care of yourself.

That time can come in a variety of ways, such as getting to the gym for a great cardio workout, spending time in meditation, or even just getting out of the office for lunch. Make a commitment to take care of yourself in meaningful and important ways, and stick to it!

But why is this sacred time so important? Because, being a manager can take a serious toll on your mental wellbeing. Not only are you dealing with the intense emotions of the people around you, but you are also giving a great deal of your emotional self to pretty much anyone who needs help. That's happening while you are managing projects, creating budgets, updating strategies, communicating up and down the management chain and across to colleagues, and everything else that anybody would ever think could possibly be your job as a manager. Whether you are managing one person or a 100-person team, that's a lot of mental energy that you need every single day.

Your brain power is exceptionally valuable not only to the people on your team and your company, but more importantly, to you. As such, you must learn to express love for yourself by nurturing your whole mental wellbeing. When you are in a managerial role that requires a great deal of conscious thought, it is important to find even just 15 minutes a day to spend sitting quietly. Just taking a few moments away from your desk and incessantly ringing phone will help calm the chaos in your head and balance your mental state.

Whether you call it meditation, sitting quietly, or a breathing exercise, you need give your brain a break. With your mind working at full tilt solving problems every hour of every day, it is no wonder that you become exhausted and emotionally raw. As you overwork your brain, consuming yourself with trying to complete every single task in front of you at the same time, your thinking will become chaotic and unfocused. Taking a few moments to sit quietly, allow your mind to let go of all the clutter, and concentrate on your breathing will vastly improve your mood and your mental wellbeing.

Meditation is simple and easy to do, and you can do it anywhere at any time, even if it is just for a few minutes during your lunch break after you have finished eating a sandwich at your desk. And just like anything worth doing, the more you practice meditating, the better you will get at it and the easier you'll be able to manage the mental stress that comes with being the responsible manager of a successful team.

While there are many ways to meditate, one of the most commonly accepted practices is to first find a comfortable chair and sit down. As you sit, be sure that both feet are relaxing comfortably on the floor and place your hands naturally into your lap. It is very important that you feel comfortable in the chair and that it is supporting your weight evenly, securely, and above all, you're seated position does not distract you in any way.

Continue to relax by closing your eyes so that you block out all visual stimulation and light. Some of us will need to turn the lights off, which is perfectly fine to do. Eliminating all other stimulation in the environment is also important, especially if you are new to meditation. You do not want to be distracted. So, if you're at the office and you need just a few minutes to sit quietly, go to a conference room, turn off the lights, and place a sign on the door that reads, “Do not disturb.” And please, leave your phone in your desk drawer or coat pocket, someplace you won’t be tempted to look at it if it rings.

If meditation just isn't for you, there are a number of other practices that can help you focus on taking care of yourself first before you take care of others. These include connecting with both your physical body and spiritual self. All three parts--mental, physical, and spiritual-- are integrated aspects of being a whole human being.

Being a manager definitely takes a lot of mental power, but it also takes a great deal of physical stamina. Think about it. Every day you run from meeting to meeting, carry your laptop everywhere, constantly go up and down stairs, and walk from one building to the next. Of course, we are leaving out leaping tall buildings with a single bound to meet your goals and manage your team like a superhero. You don't need to be in shape like Superman or Wonder Woman, but you will need a lot of physical energy to be at the top of your game. The best way to attain this energy is simply to get—and stay—in shape.

Exercising to build your physical stamina can involve just about any activity—from working out in the gym to playing catch with your kids, or even walking to lunch instead of driving. Bottom-line, you need to be able to physically perform your duties as manager, and if you are finding yourself fatigued by the end of the day (as many of us do), you need to find a way to get your blood flowing. While managerial duties will be anything from working at a desk all day to managing the flow up and down a manufacturing line, if you find your work to be physically taxing and are completely exhausted before the day is through, you are holding your team back.

Take some time and honestly assess your current physical health to determine if it aligns with the duties you're responsible for each day. Hire a trainer if you need to, but learn what your physical limits are and start from there. Don't push yourself too hard; you are trying to be healthy, not an Olympian.

Then, develop a physical fitness plan that matches the tone and tenor of the role that you need to perform. You should include things like getting enough sleep, eating the right types of foods, and a weekly exercise regime. Don't use the copout that you need to spend time with family, so you never have time to take care of yourself. That's an easy excuse. You do have time to take care of yourself; you just need to create a plan and then stick to it. You can always invite the family along to run through the park, right? Having a physical fitness plan is first and foremost an expression of love for yourself, which is critical to your ability to be an effective manager for others. If you don't love and respect yourself, who will?

Below, find a short list of healthy activities that you can participate in to help you develop your physical fitness plan:

- Run around the park with your kids
- Walk or bike ride to and from work
- Use the stairs, rather than the elevator
- Walk to lunch instead of driving
- Bring a healthy lunch from home and go outside to eat
- Eat half of what the restaurant provides and take in the rest home for another meal
- Establish a weightlifting regimen — back and biceps, chest and triceps, shoulders and biceps,

legs, and one entire workout dedicated just your arms

- Set up your desk ergonomically, which includes having the right chair

- Go rock climbing

- Swim laps around a pool or lake

- Take your dog to the beach and play Frisbee

- Select produce from the market of multiple different colors

- Snack on vegetables, rather than cookies

- Eat more protein and fiber rather than filling up on crackers

These are just a few of the ideas to get you started on a healthier physical outlook. As with all health matters, consult your physician. Doctors are exceptionally good at helping you determine what you should be doing on a physical basis to strengthen your body. Your physician can also refer you to nutritionists, who can help you determine the right nutritional plan to produce the results you seek, which in the end will help you successfully fulfill your role as a manager. (And live a long, happy, and healthy life.)

Whatever you do, get out there and make it work for yourself so that you have the physical stamina that your team and others around you can rely on.

Similar to the physical plan that you develop for yourself, it is equally important to have a spiritual plan. Regardless of your spiritual beliefs, what we all seem to seek from our spirituality is a sure path for creating a better life for our loved ones and ourselves. Whether you believe in a higher power or your faith lies in pragmatism, your spiritual wellbeing is just as important as your physical and emotional health. This is not to say that any belief or faith is right and another wrong, but simply that grounding yourself in a set of fundamental ideas will provide clear direction on how to create the life you wish to live.

One spiritual practice that can fit for most anyone is the process of identifying personal aspirations. This process is not meant to stand in for any strongly held religious beliefs. This is simply meant to get you thinking deeply about the things you aspire to change in your life, or the person you aspire to become. It is safe to say this is a living, breathing process that will change as much as you do. Try not to be too hard on yourself, this is not meant to expose your flaws as a human being. This is a very personal exercise that is meant to help you find the strength within yourself to become the person you wish to be.

To get to your simple list of personal aspirations, spend time thinking deeply about many of the lessons you've learned in this book. Below, you'll find a list of questions that you can ask yourself to help you determine your aspirations, based on the exact type of manager you would like to become. Ask yourself these questions:

Personal Aspirations Questionnaire	
What do I want to stop doing?	
What do I want to start doing?	
What do I need to do less of?	
What do I need to more of?	
What do I want to do?	
What should I do?	
What am I doing?	
How do I want to spend my time?	
How do I want others to perceive me?	

Create Affirmation Statements

From this list, you will be able to see themes from which you can create a set of affirmation statements that will guide you in becoming the type of manager that you want to be. You might even find a few aspirations that relate to your personal or family life; those are good ones to keep as part of this list because they will likely help you find balance in your life, too.

Create an affirmation statement by simply writing the sentence as if exists today. For example, think about the above question, "How do I want others to perceive me?" Let's say you answered, "Others perceive me as exceptionally knowledgeable." So then, your affirmation statement would be, "Others perceive me as exceptionally knowledgeable." Yup! It's seriously that easy.

Below, you will find a list of affirmation statements that you can use to customize your list or use as inspiration to develop new statements that are specifically for you.

Example Affirmation Statements for People Managers:

- I am in control of my emotional reactions.
- I have exceptionally mature business relationships with others.
- I offer comfort to my team through professional support and compassion.
- The people on my team have a great deal of faith in my managerial abilities and follow my leadership confidently.
- I am a successful manager who others look to as the example of what a manager of people should be.
- My management hierarchy looks at me as the most innovative manager they have on their team.
- I wow my team with my ability to be professional and caring.

- I have the right people on my team to help me successfully run our business.

- Managing projects through effective delegation excites me.

- I am surrounded by people who help me succeed each and every day.

- My team is the premier group in our entire business organization, as a result of my effective management.

- I am an intuitive manager who makes wise decisions.

- I use my exceptionally well-developed relationships with my team members to produce exceptionally impactful business results.

- I give myself permission to be me and never allow myself to be a corporate hack.

- I am patient and kind and people sincerely like me.

This list is not comprehensive, but it should get you started on your own. We know from experience that you can achieve exceptionally good results by creating a list of aspirations and sticking to them on a regular basis. In some ways, it's the same practice as a business strategy, except that it becomes your strategy as a manager to be an exceptional human being and leader of people.

If you decide to employ this spiritual tactic in your own life, draft your unique list of aspirations, print it out, and keep it with you at all times. At some point in each day, pull out your list and speak your aspirations out loud so your intentions comingle with the energy around you.

For this method to be effective, you must believe the aspirations you have written are true, even if they have not manifested in your life just yet. When you employ this practice honestly, you will soon see that the aspirations you desire are in fact truly who you are.

To learn more about this practice, which some spiritual leaders call prayer and others call the "the law of attraction," refer to your local bookstore or spiritual center. There are a number of books on the subject that will help you put these principals into action.

Happy + Healthy = Productive

Now that you have a plan for your mental, physical, and spiritual selves and have begun to develop these practices in your life, you should start to feel happier and healthier than you have ever felt before. This is because you created a conscious plan that you can stick to and a regimen that has become ingrained in your life. And, when you know that your needs are fully taken care of, you can apply your own special brand of help to those people around you by focusing on their individual and specific needs.

Start to plan exactly how you feel best able to help those people around you. You may address some or all of their personal aspects, including mental, physical, and emotional. For example, you may have a number of people on your team who are not eating right. It happens. Especially when you have a team that is exceptionally productive. With this situation, often they will sit at their desk through the lunch hour and feverously type away on keyboard while mindlessly munching a cheeseburger. This means that they are committed to getting everything done so they can produce the type of results they expect of themselves. Unfortunately, this type of behavior will only help someone burn out exceptionally fast.

In fact, burnout is one of your biggest adversaries as a manager. It will suck the health right out of every employee. Burnout will take the happy-go-lucky person on your team and turn their smile upside down right into a nasty frown. Most managers who are saddled with a team that experiences an immense amount of burnout will have to deal with this, pronto. If they don't, their team members will disappear—one by one. Burnout happens because a manager does not focus on helping his or her people avoid this time killer and allows hyper-productivity to trump a healthy work environment.

There are a number of activities that you can employ as a manager to help your team avoid burnout, including:

- Delegate responsibility and then agree to the delegate's decisions.

- Schedule team lunches away from the office so the team has an opportunity to interact with one another socially.

- Insist that the team's productivity stops by 6 PM each and every night.

- Avoid responding to e-mails that come to you in the evening so that your employees do not feel they must answer e-mails all night to keep up with you.

- Avoid sending and responding to e-mail on the weekends.

- Talk to your employees about your non-work interests, family, children, and friends, and invite your employees to do the same.

- Be real about the workload and honestly tell your employees that your team is experiencing heavy productivity at the moment and their hard work will pay off soon.

- Thank your employees all the time, not just once in a while for the work that you expect to be done, but for anything that was not expected of them.

- When an issue comes up, be transparent about it and ask your team for help in solving the issue.

These are just a few ideas to get you started helping your team. Your next step is to write a plan that helps your employees lead a happy, healthy, productive life. To do that, you'll need to develop an individual plan for each and every person on your team. The plan should include your role in how you will support that individual to be successful and avoid burnout.

Now, here's the kicker: not everyone is going to want your help. As a matter fact, some people will live their entire life being miserable, dreaming of the life they could live if they were to be happy, healthy, and productive. Not everyone is going to achieve it, mostly because of their own personal limitations that they set upon themselves. But as their manager, with the plan that you have created for each individual member on your team, you will be able to help them when they are ready to ask for it.

Not everyone will ask for help, but when they do, be ready. As a manager, you should be prepared with an individual plan to help any employee at any time. During your one-on-one meetings you can advise the employee that you see they are indeed stressed out, and that it may even be affecting their work. Give them an example of how you overcame this type of situation.

Talk to them about a time when you were stressed out and explain how you overcame that stress.

Even if they agree with you, some employees will never directly let you know of their plight. Some may never exhibit the signs of stress, but that doesn't mean that you should ignore what is clear to you. It's your responsibility as their manager to bring it up during a discussion. You don't want burnout to be the bane of your department.

The most important point here is that no one will accept the help that you're providing unless they want it. So, again, it's exceptionally important to act as a role model because an employee's ability to succeed at their job is greatly influenced by what their manager is expecting of them, whether that is a specific and direct expectation or a perceived expectation that is based on the type of behavior that the manager exhibits. So, if you're demonstrating a great deal of stress to your employees, they may think that stress is what you want them to be experiencing, or that you would be unwilling to help them with their stressful moments because you experience a great deal of stress yourself.

Be a friend and offer help, but don't push your help on others if they don't want it. You can only help those who ask for it. But, as a conscientious manager, you should be prepared with a plan when one of your team members does decide to ask for help. This is important so that you are fully available to them when they seek out your assistance.

Even when you have employees who ask for help, they may not want the help you offer them. Or, maybe they do want your help, but they are just incapable or unable to dedicate themselves to the behavioral changes necessary for them to live a happy and healthy and productive life. Be very aware of your abilities and your limitations; some of your employee's problems may just be out of your league. In that case, give them your support and compassion and offer to assist them in finding the help they need.

You simply will not be able to help everyone with all of their problems, and listening hour after hour to the same issue over and over again, especially if that person is not willing to make significant changes, is a big waste of your time. Always remember that you are a manager of people at a business and not a trained counselor. (Even if you are a trained counselor or psychological therapy in the workplace, this is not part of your job description.) Your role is to drive high performance. Yes, sometimes that means listening to people's issues and helping resolve them so that you can return to your role of driving performance within your team. But, when you have an employee who is constantly seeking your help, needing your approval, or is otherwise wrapped up in behaviors that are in conflict with their work, there may be nothing you can do, except to separate yourself from this employee and their issues. Does that mean fire the employee? No. Does that mean transfer the employee to a new team? No. In that case, you'd only be transferring the problem someone else.

What this does mean, however, is that you can discontinue your efforts in helping solve this employee's problems. As a matter of fact, you will want to have a tactful conversation with the employee to suggest that he or she start to see a therapist or other health professional about their issues, since it's not something you are able as their manager to help resolve. It's okay to direct an employee to someone who can help them.

Within all of the relationships you will have with your employees, there is an amazingly positive source of energy and compassion that can lead to you to success and that source is you. When you are happy and healthy, and that is the core of who you are, even in the most difficult of situations you will have a wealth of opportunities to give help to your team when they need it and in a way that they can use it, while respecting yourself and your individual needs as well. Always focus on your personal wellbeing first, so that you can help others to live productive lives, too.

Personal wellbeing clearly comes in many forms and not all practices are right for everyone. Some of us will thoroughly enjoy taking time out once a day to meditate, while others will hit the gym, and still others may want to spend time outdoors connecting in with nature. And while it is best to have a program that supports your mental, physical and spiritual wellbeing, you'll find what works best for you. Once you've got your own program in place, and you are practicing wellness on a daily basis, you'll see that your life will be far happier, healthier, and much more productive. The benefits of a balanced wellness program aren't just for you; these benefits will also wash over your team. Taking care of yourself first gives you all of the time, patience, love, and kindness you need to take care of others later. If you don't have a wellness plan in place today, put one in place right away. After all, you can only have an effective relationship with others if you have one with yourself first.

***Know When It's Time to Go

All good things must come to an end, and your job is no different. There are a hundred reasons to leave a job, but most managers, like all employees, tend to leave a job because of their relationship with their manager, rather than the job itself or the team they've built. Still, some will leave because they are not earning a high enough salary, the benefits are weak or have been reduced, there is no opportunity to grow a career, or the company is about to go under. Regardless of your reason for wanting to get out, the most important thing you can do for yourself and your career is to recognize the warning signs and plan your exit before your negative emotions start to affect your behavior, which is a normal human response to problematic situations. Why? Because all of the work you put into building effective employee relationships can be wiped out with an exit that is anything but elegant, graceful ,and radiating with respect for those who will stay with the company.

Knowing the warning signs, however, can be tough for most of us. One day you are in love with the job, your team, and the company, and the very next day you wake up with the realization that something is amiss. The lucky few of you will know exactly what the issue is, while others will spend a few sleepless nights and grumpy days trying to figure it all out. To help you determine what your warnings signs are, ask yourself these questions:

- Do I like what I am doing?
- Do I have a good relationship with my manager?
- Does my team respect me?

- Do I respect my team?
- What do I like to do?
- What do I hate to do?
- What am I doing on a daily basis?
- If I could change anything about this job, what would it be?
- Why do I get grumpy at work?
- Why am I so frustrated with this job?
- Am I being compensated fairly for my contributions?

The questions are very simple and the answers are likely already swimming around in your head and have been for some time. As a matter of fact, you already answered similar questions about your positive and negative emotions in an earlier chapter. But, like most of us, you need to spend time asking thoughtful questions to sort through the clutter and get to the truth. When it comes times to consider making a job change, we recommend taking time to critically consider the issues that you are facing each and every day. It's important to move those issues out of the emotional aspect of your consciousness and into the rational side of your brain.

If the signs are all pointing to a quick exit, pay close attention to be sure you are making the best move for yourself. In business today, there is very little loyalty, and a company will fire you, lay you off, or change the terms of your employment agreement in a heartbeat if it serves the company. Contrary to what the U.S. Congress determined in 2011, corporations are not people, and they cannot be loyal, show love, or offer you anything more than what you have agreed to. Companies cannot make you happy, and if you want to be happy and need to get out of a job, do it. Now, of course, it is always advisable to first work on resolving the issues that are standing in the way of your happiness at your current job, but if it is clear that the differences are irreconcilable, get out fast!

If you are planning on leaving your job, remember to put yourself first--in every decision you make. Assuming most of us are very good people, we will tend to put the company first in our decision making. We'll focus on what we need to do to leave our position in a way that offers continued success, and an amicable separation, and that's admirable. But, don't compromise on your principles if you are leaving a role that is no longer serving you. You are your highest priority once you've decided to take action and exit a company.

When you do decide to leave, however, leave for the right reasons, such as:

- More money
- Career advancement
- Better work-life balance
- Shorter commute
- Better benefits
- Nicer manager
- Bigger or more interesting responsibilities

Leaving for all of the right reasons means that everyone around you will understand your point of view and more willingly help you transition away from your old job and into your new job with dignity. Now there are always a number of bad bosses who will try to do everything in their power to make you feel small for moving along; but again, if you put yourself first in your transition, then none of that will matter. What does matter is that you will be moving on to a role that offers you the type of opportunities that are important to you, and that will add happiness to your life at work, home, and play.

The most common reason a person anywhere in the world leaves a job is because his or her manager just sucks. And when you have a poor relationship with your manager, it will manifest in many different undesirable ways that will cause you ultimately to leave your job. Perhaps your manager never says thank you, doesn't value your contributions, or sets obstacles in your way to success. Or, perhaps you are both bull-headed, strong-willed personalities and the office just isn't big enough for the two of you.

Once you have made the decision to leave, it's important that you do so with dignity and grace, in a way that helps your manager to grow, and in a manner that helps the company to understand the exact reasons why you are leaving. If you leave a company because of a manager, you must be explicitly clear about the fact that this person is the cause for you leaving your job. However, to ensure you are protecting your own personal reputation when you leave, be sure to maintain mature relationships and offer your criticisms of your manager constructively.

This is not an easy task, because for most of us, the process of deciding to leave a job creates a great deal of emotional energy. By allowing yourself to be emotionally available and honest is important. You want to remain human throughout this process.

The following is a process through which you can start to understand the reasons you are leaving and also help your manager grow and allow the company to support that growth. Take the time to carefully address these steps by honestly expressing yourself.

1. *Be honest with your manager:* If you're leaving your job because of your manager, he or she needs to know the reason or reasons why you are leaving. Youthful managers will try to talk to you about the relationship that you have developed together, and even attempt to rectify any of the bad blood that may exist between the two of you. These less-evolved managers tend to get emotionally upset, and perhaps even yell at you for being so honest about why you are leaving the post. If your relationship with your manager can be fixed, then perhaps you can still work for him or her in the organization. If that isn't an option, you may find a new job in the company reporting to someone else. When you talk to your manager about your reasons for leaving, he or she should not be surprised. As a professional, you must have the tenacity to confront this type of negative relationship head on. This is so that when you do find yourself in the precarious situation of needing to resign because of the tenuous relationship you have, your manager will understand that there are irreconcilable differences between the two of you and likely just let you move on to your next role in the world.

2. *Be honest in your resignation letter:* In most countries a resignation letter is required to confirm in writing that you are voluntarily leaving your job. Oftentimes, these resignation letters simply express the last day of employment that you intend to

provide to your company. However, when you're leaving a job because of your manager, document the reasons you are leaving the organization and the steps that you took to resolve the conflict with your manager. It's important to point out the successes and milestones you have had in the job, too. By using this formula, you are providing the company an opportunity to understand the exact reasons you are leaving the job, and also stating how you are a valuable team player who has fueled the success of the company in a number of different ways. Finally, you are being a mature professional by attempting to resolve the relationship issues up front. A lot of people find this approach to be very risky. After all, it puts all of your sentiments in writing, and no one wants to burn bridges. However, what you are doing here, in a constructive and professional way, is being very respectful to your employers so they are able to understand that you have a legitimate reason for leaving the company. This is also a sign that you have a great deal of self-respect and are unwilling to be mistreated in the workplace.

3. *Be honest during your exit interview:* Many companies will ask to meet with you on your final day of employment so you can return company-issued equipment, have an opportunity to talk about your reasons for leaving the company, and resolve any conflicts that may still be present. Many HR professionals will let you believe this session is all about giving you that opportunity to express your dissatisfaction with the business. Consider how best to utilize this time with your HR professional so you can express the experience you had with your manager. Be prepared to let HR know what you did to resolve the relationship issues, and be available to them after you leave if they need more information from you. All too often, the HR team is

highly aware of those managers who are inadequate, but can only apologize for the manager's behavior. Please note that it is only your role to express what you did to resolve the situation and offer to help them the future. This signals to HR that you're fully committed to the company now and also in the future, regardless of your employment status.

This type of exit will help you remain in the good graces of the company, effectively keeping that bridge from burning. This method will also offer you the opportunity to be exceptionally honest with who you are as a person and why the situation did not work for you. If you use this model, it can be a win-win situation. It is highly important that you express everything that you need to during this termination process so you do not carry any negative feelings into your next role.

HR will often claim that people are leaving a company due to career development reasons. Whether that claim is fact or fiction, it is an exceptionally good reason for you to leave your job. After all, if you don't manage your career, no one is going to do it for you.

As a manager, career development rarely, if ever, is achieved simply through a better title or larger salary. Career development in your organization should be an opportunity to acquire new knowledge, develop new skills, or expand your abilities. Don't focus on the next title, the corner office, or more people reporting to you. In the interest of your ongoing career in management, seek different opportunities to get experience early on in your career, rather than just trying to quickly being named vice president.

For a number of reasons, it is a mistake to go for the high level titles when you don't have the right experience. For example, people will discredit you in the role, you won't have enough time "in the chair" to understand the nuances of leadership (even if you have exceptionally good skills), and you will always be stuck in the job that you are in if you have an inflated title. That's because no other company will be interested in bringing on an employee who has a job title by name but has not earned the experience of high-level leadership in their organization. Be wary of companies that want to give you exceptionally large titles for the type of experience you have after only a few years in the job.

Experience is just an accumulation of the many successes and mistakes one has made throughout his or her career. If you are interested in truly developing your career, learn from others, rather than just quickly jumping from title to title. However, the progression of your career development with any company must match your own desired pace of development. That means if you are stuck in a company that is very slow to offer new job experiences, mentorships, classroom training, or perhaps doesn't offer any formal programs, be aware that the opportunity for you to advance your career within that company will be stunted. Nobody wants that.

If career development is truly the reason you intend to leave your job, be sure that you first explore what your current employer can do to you to grow your career in the direction you seek. For example, if you believe that you need to learn new programming languages to remain relevant for the next five years, be sure that you investigate learning opportunities at your present company before you resign. Better yet, ask your current employer to pay for the type of development you are seeking so that you can then bring those skills back to your workplace and deliver greater success for the company. No, you don't need to be in an organization forever. As a matter of fact, many CEOs will tell you that you should not be in a job more than 10 years; however, seeing the marketplace realistically, it is likely that a person will remain in a job for two to five years, depending on the type of experience that they're having.

But, don't be fooled by some crafty recruiter's remarks that tell you to stay in a job for at least three to five years. Your career is your career. That means you get to decide exactly how you want to develop it, in which direction you want to take your future, and specifically how you want to get there. As a matter of fact, spend some time looking at some of the most senior executives resumes in your organization and see how long they've stayed in a given role, company, or industry. You'll likely find they have moved around just as much as you have. Keep in mind, these types of comments from recruiters are just meant to give them the upper hand. Don't let that scare you or hold you back from developing your career.

Again, give your company the opportunity to invest in you and offer to bring those skills back to their organization to fuel its success. If the company doesn't have the time, money, or power to invest in you, then it is likely that your career aspirations don't match the company's current trajectory and it is a good idea to leave. Of course, you should always be honest about your reasons for departing from a role. And in this case, if the place is a good place to work, you may want to leave their employ to develop your career and return in a few years into a more senior role, once you have the type of experiences that the company seeks for their higher-level employees. That's another win-win situation.

Another very good reason to leave your role is for financial reasons. Each of our circumstances in life is different. Some of us have a large number of kids to support, a spouse, a home, and other financial obligations as simple as student loans or a car payment. However, as an employee of an organization, the salary that you were hired with may not be sufficient enough for you as your life evolves over time. So, if you are not making enough money in the job that you are currently working in, it may be time to leave for an organization that is able and willing to pay you in a way that meets your needs.

Regardless of your financial needs, you may also leave the role because you are underpaid for the type of work that you are providing or the skills you bring to the organization, and you feel the company undervalues that. This is another great reason to have a clear understanding of your industry and what you offer to your organization. Know the financial value of the type of work you do not only within your company but also the market in general. If you are considering a departure because you are underpaid, gather your facts from industry information and credible career sites so you can speak about the wage disparity intelligently and with authority. In other words, a quick Google search for a statistic or graph will not cut it; be sure to do your due diligence and create an argument for yourself as to why you deserve to make more money.

Whatever your financial reason may be, if you are not making enough in an organization to feel good about the work you're doing, then it's probably time to leave. After all, financial security is one of those basic human emotions that must be satisfied as a result of your hard work and dedication to yourself and your family. Financial security gives everyone a sense of control. So, if you have decided to leave your organization because of a financial inequity, then do so in a way that makes sense and with a new job that pays you what you know you are worth.

First, give your manager and opportunity to give you a raise. If you know that you are underpaid, present the reliable data you researched. Consider requesting salary information from HR to show you are not receiving an equitable payment, compared to other folks in your organization. When you do this, you give your manager the opportunity to rectify the issue, which is probably an issue that your manager may not be thinking about or paying close attention to, since most managers don't usually deal with salary issues except for once or twice a year. Also, this gives your manager another opportunity to point out to you what he or she expects for the type of pay you are requesting. If those two points of view don't line up, then again that just signals to you that it's the right time to leave the organization.

You deserve to make the money you have worked hard to rightfully earn. You will work for different companies in different positions before your skills and experience line up with the title and salary you seek. If you're looking for a raise, ask for one, but do it in a way that is respectful to you, to your manager, and to the success of your company.

HR also identifies culture as a theme to represent why people leave a given company.

However, is it culture—the language, actions, and icons that make up the company—or is it something else within the interactions of its people that cause employees to leave companies? It's important to note here that you can certainly tell your manager and HR that the company culture is why you're leaving the organization. But for your own sake, figure out what it was about the language, actions, and icons within the company that created your discomfort and need to change companies. You want to be sure you fit into a company culture so you can succeed. Determine what's important to you and seek that out.

For most organizations, icons are going to be relatively innocuous because they need to have appeal to large groups of people. And, the language that the organization uses is usually well scripted by internal communications professionals or Public Relations departments. In either case, the message that they send is going to be one of positivity and optimism about the future, rather than the straight shooting reality that a manager would likely express to his or her team.

Where most people get frustrated, especially managers who are playing the middle position, is when the language doesn't match the actions of a company. More times than not, a manager is saddled with delivering negative news about any number of situations that doesn't match how the company communicates as an organization. So for example, managers are often given the task of announcing that bonuses are underfunded while the company is boasting about its expanded growth year-over-year. Those two things just don't match up, and it doesn't make it any easier for manager to play his or her role.

Another reason that people leave organizations is that they just don't like the people they work with. Companies attract a certain profile that they believe to be important to getting the job done. Some companies are highly competitive and seek to hire extremely aggressive people, which means that very little gets done unless you have the stamina to beat your teammates at the competitive game, rather than working together as one holistic team across the entire company to get something done. This is a very common practice for un-evolved organizations that seek to drive internal competitiveness as a means to weed out the lower performing employees, rather than recognizing that there is a great deal of variance in how people work in the workplace and that teamwork is often valued by a large number of people, rather than pure competition.

Regardless of your cultural reason for moving on from an organization, the most important point is to move fast. You will frustrate yourself, bring negativity home, and generally have a less healthy life if you continue working in a culture that is inconsistent with your personal values and expectations. It's important to ask the right questions up front in terms of deciding if a company culture is right for you. Otherwise, you will be conflicted internally, which will eventually lead you right out the same door you came in.

Leave with Confidence

Regardless of your reason for leaving, leave with confidence, once you've made the decision, and transition in a way that not only respects the company that has employed you, but also respects the people that you're leaving behind, many of whom may be upset that you are leaving them in the dust.

Being a manager is one of the hardest things you'll ever do in your life, as well as one of the most rewarding experiences you can ever have. When you are an exceptional manager, you will be sought out by companies and have an endless list of valuable career opportunities open to you. Know yourself, know your team, know your job, and know when to get out. If you know all this exceptionally well, you will live a life that is happy, healthy, and productive now and far into the future.

Managing Success is Entirely Up to You

By now you've got to be scratching your head, wondering why pretty much everything you think, say, and do as a manager has such a big impact on employees. Well, it does. It's just that simple, and if you don't agree just yet, sit back and consider the following.

Managers have a huge responsibility, much larger than executive leaders, in that they are responsible for the human interactions that occur up, down, and across an organization. You sit in the middle of all of these humans, coordinate their actions, serve as a communications hub, and push everyone to deliver on time and on budget. So while you may look at the individual parts of the manager's role and think that you only really want to focus on being good in one area, it is far more important to see the big picture and commit to the specific actions that produce effective employee relationships. To do that, you have to commit to being a good manager and not a bad boss.

To commit, you've first go to know yourself exceptionally well. You'll never be able to have massively effective relationships with anyone if you don't know yourself first, let alone your employees. Be clear about your management style, emotions, and motivations. If you discovered that you need to make tweaks to any of those, do it—right away! You are your source for unprecedented managerial success, so double down on developing yourself into the person you want to be and don't stop until you look in the mirror and beam with pride at the person you've become… and never stop improving yourself.

If it wasn't a big enough job to take on just the development of yourself, you also have so many tasks to complete in your managerial role. You could soon become overwhelmed. But don't; just take it one step at a time. The best rule of thumb is to first get the work done that is important to the people around you first, namely your employees, manager, and cross-functional teammates. And through all of this you can expect to be confronted with massive obstacles, and be expected to overcome them quickly and easily. That is an all too common experience in management.

It is in your ability to build effective employee relationships that fuel your ability to be massively successful in any managerial role you decide to take. In walking away from this book, we hope that you understand this simple point: To actually achieve this effectiveness in your relationships with employees, you have to let your humanity shine through and always, always, always recognize that everyone around you is a human too...with the same emotions, motivations, obstacles, influences, and desire for meaning , as you.

So go forward, put the advice we presented here into practice, and build effective employee relationships. When you do this well, you will experience all of the love, joy, and surprise that management has to offer. It's an amazing journey and you deserve nothing less than fantastic results.

Congratulations! You're well on your way to being the best manager that any of us have ever had in our entire career.

Works Cited

Hill, Napoleon. *How to Sell Your Way Through Life*. Hoboken: John Wiley & Sons, 1939. Book.

Leaders, Leadership Now: Building a Community of. *Quotes on Management*. LeadershipNow / M2 Communications, 1996-2009. Internet.

Meyer, Paul. *Attitude is Everything*. The Leading Edge Publishing Company, 2006. Book.

Parrott, W. G. *Emotions in Social Psychology*. Philadelphia: Psychology Press, 2000. Book.

Pavlina, Steve. *List of Values* . Unknown: www.StevePavlina.com, Unknown. Internet. <www.StevePavlina.com>.

Quotes, Brainy. *Brainy Quotes*. Unknown: BookRags Media Network, 2001. Internet. <www.brainyquote.com>.

Index

About the Author

Jeremy Henderson is the Chief Client Partner and Founder of Jungle Red Communication, a corporate human relations consulting firm that focusing on helping its clients build happy, healthy, productive workplaces that deliver tangible business results through internal communication, leadership, decision making, and corporate social structures. He helps executives and managers to become massively effective and helps organizations build high-performance teams, renew corporate cultures, and design programs that increase employee satisfaction and steward change.

He has worked for some of the most impressive and innovative companies of our time, including Razorfish, Salesforce.com, eBay, VeriSign, and City Colleges of Chicago—Europe. While at Jungle Red Communication, his clients have included companies as small as 30 employees working out of one office and as massive as 55,000 employees globally. These clients have included creative services agencies, social networking companies, technology industry leaders, and a well-known sports and entertainment organization.

His firmly held social belief that if employees experience a great workplace, one that is happy and healthy, then they will be more productive; and when they are more productive, they will go home and have a happier home life; and when they have a happy home life, then their families will go out into the community and cultivate better relationships; and when we have better relationships across our communities, then our society succeeds.

Made in the USA
San Bernardino, CA
20 April 2013